Running for Good:
The Fiona Oakes Story

BY **FIONA OAKES**

Foreword

In 2012 I went to the Sahara to run the gruelling Marathon des Sables for the first time. For those who don't know this it is an extreme 250km self-sufficient race over 7 days in the desert. There were over 800 competitors that year and it's impossible to get to know everyone. Therefore I wasn't aware that also taking part in the race was a very special lady by the name of Fiona Oakes. The reason I say this is because taking part in this race was the choice I made in my life that eventually led me to getting to know her, and also to be influenced by her.

The Marathon des Sables was part of a life-changing journey for me, like it is for many people. It so happened that after this race I eventually left a lucrative and successful career in the City to begin the difficult life of an entrepreneur.

I had been the co-owner of an independent niche running shop in Essex, UK, for about a year or so, when I first met Fiona in person. Her partner Martin had called beforehand to make an appointment. Through the door burst a small woman and in her hand was a tiny bear named Percy. She wasn't tall but she was clearly very fit and strong and she had this energy about her which is difficult to describe. She was dressed in boot-cut jeans, trainers and a T-shirt. It seemed like she had rushed to get there. She explained she worked running an animal sanctuary. She still had dirt under her nails and I noticed her strong hands and forearms. She was delicate and tough at the same time.

A contradiction. I had to focus to keep up with her pace as she wouldn't stop talking. She needed some gear for her next race in another remote desert.

Because of her tiny build it was difficult but we managed to find an old sample model of a backpack that suited her. She said she was vegan and it was difficult to not get caught by her strong conviction and passion for this cause. Where other people would choose down products to minimise the weight of the material they carry, Fiona would go for a synthetic sleeping bag and jacket and carry at least three times the weight and volume but it didn't faze her. This wasn't about her, this was about the animals.

I still to this day know Fiona as a contradiction. She will tell you that she is stocky, that she is an average runner, that she does or is nothing special.

Let me tell you though that Fiona is one of the most remarkable and extraordinary people I have ever met. She is just very humble and she never brags about anything. Yet, what she has achieved is something that very few people do as you will realise when you read her story.

Despite a severe knee injury she suffered at a young age, she has run marathons faster than what most well-trained men could, she holds several world records, and she works tirelessly for animal welfare, something which she has done since the age of three when she decided to become a vegetarian and subsequently a vegan.

Fiona was part of my inspiration when I decided to ditch meat for reasons of health, athletic performance, environment and animal welfare. This may not be your thing but regardless of your beliefs I urge you to read Fiona's story. Her strong sense of empathy, compassion, respect, selflessness, and responsibility are ethical values we could all learn from and adopt in our own lives.

Elisabet Barnes

Coach, endurance runner and 2x winner of Marathon des Sables

Contents

Foreword.. iii

1.   Prologue 1

2.   Formations... 3

3.   The Stumbling Block... 8

4.   Cycling and the Sanctuary..................................... 19

5.   The Start of a Marathon 25

6.   Fire Crew.. 32

7.   A Reason for Action... 37

8.   Freedom to Run 41

9.   Vegan Runner.. 47

10.   Full-On Marathons and Training 53

11.   Training to Win 60

12.   Base Preparations 70

13.   Impact.. 77

14.   Rovaniemi.. 80

15.   The Great North Run 85

16. Finland to Dartmoor...89

17. Marathon des Sables 92

18. Day to Day Misery 101

19. The Rescue 106

20. Reflections 111

21. A Pull North 117

22. Going North...120

23. The North Pole 123

24. Coverage 131

25. An Around-the-World World Record 133

26. The Volcano Marathon 143

27. The Antarctic Ice Marathon.....................................150

28. The End of Antarctica 161

29. The Holidays...171

30. Marathon des Sables Redux......................................175

31. The Rio Marathon 189

32. Seven-Seven-Seven 194

33. Race to the Stones (in a Cow Suit)............................202

34. The 4 Deserts 216

35. Percy Bear 223

CHAPTER 1

Prologue

I REMEMBER BEING IN HOSPITAL for a long stretch of time. It was September, but it was extremely hot. What I remember most strongly from that time is it being so hot and being stuck in my bed. They'd given me a narrow bed, but I was near a window. And my poor mum, who isn't horsey, and doesn't feel comfortable around large animals, she'd been and fetched Max, my pony, all the way from where he was kept at this farm and walked him all the way to the hospital.

I just turned over one day and I saw him. I couldn't go out because I had a big wound from the operation and I was prone to infection. But she got him there, and I remember that was just the most amazing thing, being able to see Max there.

I won't lie and say the sight inspired me so much that I laid there and vowed that one day I was going to be an athlete running races to support animals. It didn't happen like that at all. It's not some big formulated plan, I'm not going to say that I knew how things would turn out.

It simply never occurred to me that I wasn't going to be able to get over it.

CHAPTER 2

Formations

I WAS A HUGE BABY WHEN I was born. My mother is not a big lady, she's only about five foot two, and I was a huge baby, born with a full head of hair. The story goes my mum's music teacher came over to see me in my pram, and she looked into the pram and she looked at my fingers and she said, 'Um. Not a pianist. Perhaps a cellist'. Because I'm short and very stocky. I'm not petite in any way, shape or form.

I had a pretty conventional upbringing in some respects. I was brought up in the north of England, in a town called Chesterfield, in Derbyshire. It was just my mum and dad, my older sister, and me. My dad was in the mining industry, and a lot of the time when I was a child he was on and off strike. My mum was a piano teacher, but she always wanted to go into nursing, and later on she actually decided to follow that dream and became a nurse.

Where my childhood got unconventional was when I went vegetarian at three years old. Then when I was six years old I decided that I wanted to go vegan. None of my family were vegetarian or vegan at the time. People are surprised at the idea of a small child deciding to go vegetarian or vegan, and I think perhaps a lot of the time people don't really believe it; they don't believe that it was just me deciding that. But the decision to go vegetarian, it wasn't really a decision, it was a reaction—an instinct: a very simple one. If you love something, you don't harm them. And I loved animals. I was passionate about animals, always have been. So to three-year-old Fiona, going vegetarian was the obvious thing to do, an instinct.

Then as I became a little older and a little more aware, the question was why do we eat other animal products, and where do they come from? Why does the chicken give us her egg? Why does the cow give us her milk? And at that point I consider myself very blessed that my mother was honest with me. She explained they don't decide to give us these things. It's something that we breed them for and we take. This came as a bombshell to me. I decided I wanted no part of that either. And that's why I became vegan, when I was six years old.

I think it would have been a lot more difficult for me had my mother not had a role model to turn to. My mother, as I mentioned, was a music teacher, and her own music teacher had been a vegan lady—which was literally unheard of in the 1950s. People didn't even know what a vegan was. They'd never heard the word at all. But my mother had kept in contact with this lady, who was able to articulate in an adult way what I was feeling in a childlike way, and explain things well enough to get my parents to allow me to continue being vegan.

So I was very fortunate in that respect, but that said, some of the hardest parts of my childhood were when I went vegetarian and vegan. My grandparents made it very difficult. They were always accusing my mum of not doing right by me, telling her that it may be all right now but she was abusing me and in the future my development and growth would be inhibited in some way. It made it very miserable for me. And the veganism caused problems when I began having trouble with my knee, slightly before my teenage years. Through going in and out of hospital I'd lost a lot of weight, not through the veganism, but through pain and the condition I had causing lots of problems for me, but it was insinuated that it was because of my vegan diet, which compounded things.

That was an incredibly challenging time for all the family actually. I don't like to dwell on it, but it was a foundational experience. I know what it's like to suffer myself, so I can relate to it with other beings, whether they're human or not. And I certainly don't want to inflict it on them unnecessarily. I know how far I can push myself and I'm prepared to experience the necessary pain myself, to reach my goals. But not for anything else. I can't stand to inflict pain, or allow pain to be inflicted, on other beings. I abhor cruelty to humans and animals alike.

I became very miserable very young at the fact that I couldn't understand why everybody didn't feel the same as I did about animals, or other people even. They just didn't seem to care.

I've never seen animals as anything but having the same individual personalities as people. It's never occurred to me that it would be any otherwise. It still doesn't make sense to me that other people don't see it in the same way. I still really can't get my head around the way that people don't relate to farm animals in the way that they do domestic animals. Like it's all right to express love for a cat or a dog, or possibly a horse. But not for a cow, a sheep, a pig, or a goat.

I remember one day as a child my family went out on a Sunday afternoon drive, and we ran over a mouse, and I went hysterical. My dad stopped the car and we went back and tried to see if anything could be done, but the mouse was dead. We buried it. The whole thing upset me deeply, but it didn't seem to bother the rest of the family like it was bothering me. Or, similarly, a few years ago I was travelling round the M25, and there was a traffic jam. My car stopped next to a pig transporter, and I was looking at this three-tiered level of pigs all marked for slaughter. I looked across and I was just welling up. I was shaking. And people in other vehicles were sitting there quite happily, just listening to the radio and chatting and laughing, windows down. I still can't really get it into my head why. If that transporter had been full of cats and dogs there would have been public outcry. There would have been absolute mass hysterics. They would have had to close the road and let them out. It wouldn't have been acceptable.

Yet when it's pigs or sheep or cattle, there just doesn't seem to be that same kind of connection. I can't understand why people don't sit back and think, 'Well, hey, this doesn't really make sense, does it?' Or is it simply they don't care? I've never understood. I've always just approached any animal I came across. Even when I was tiny. I was just always very bold around animals. And perhaps even now, that's when I feel at my most comfortable. With people probably not so much. But with animals it's an immediate connection.

As a child, I wouldn't say I was a loner, but I didn't have friends with the same interests, and by extension I spent a lot of my time alone. The things that excited other kids didn't excite me. My sister didn't want to play the kind of games I wanted to play. She was much more the traditional idea of a girl, wanted to play with dolls and put makeup on and all. And that wasn't me in the slightest. I wanted to be out there rough and tumble and running about. I was extremely sporty. And quite unkempt, as I probably still am. For me it was about being out in the wild. Spending time with animals. I loved that. It was just all about animals to me, all my life. I think it always will be. And I've always been interested in how they behave and how they interact with us. That's always been my passion.

In terms of individual animals, ponies have always been my thing. In fact I lost my first pony, Max, the pony I had when I was a child, on May 14, 2010. And it was absolutely devastating. This wasn't a pony, this was my best friend, the kind of friend that you spend all your time with. And they want to spend their time with you. It would just fill me with joy to see him. It was an incredible bond that we had. And when I lost him it was like losing part of myself. There have been lots of animals in my life but probably Mr. Max was the deepest connection, because he was with me for so long, well over 30 years. He died in my arms here at the sanctuary. He was incredibly special to me.

CHAPTER 3

The Stumbling Block

I WAS IN HOSPITAL FOR much of my teenage years.

When the problem with my right knee first started, everyone dismissed it as growing pains. I would say 'No, but it's really painful', and the response was 'Yes, I know, but they're really bad growing pains'. Then I started missing school because I couldn't walk. I'd be walking along and then suddenly be on the floor.

Once everyone was convinced it was more than growing pains, the doctors thought it was something called chondromalacia patella, which affects sporty kids. It's a condition where the cartilage on the underside of the knee breaks down and the knee and femur bones rub together and cause pain. So I went into hospital continually having the back of my knee caps scraped off, or having the ligaments and things readjusted around my kneecaps, to kind of pivot it in a different direction. And nothing was working. I was in and out of hospital, having operations over and over.

I had about seventeen operations in all, back and forth from one leg to the other leg, trying to correct things without doing anything too drastic. Then my left leg started to pack up, then the right leg again. So one strange thing about my right leg is I don't actually grow any hair from it. It is completely bald, and that is because of the amount of time I was in plaster when I was adolescent. The hair just stopped growing. My leg was just in the dark all the time, and that killed its capacity, apparently, to grow hair. I was in and out of hospital, in and out, in and out. All that time. It was just horrible. Awful.

Then because I compensated and relied so heavily on my left leg, that started to fail me in a similar sort of way. It wasn't as drastic as what I had on my right side, not as bad, but I did have corrective surgeries for the tendons and muscles that hold the knee joint in place. They were all aligned differently. I had four or five operations on my left leg, and the main bulk on my right.

The routine was, I'd have an operation. I'd be put into plaster, because at the time the school of thought was 'Immobilise the leg. Don't allow them to bend it. Don't allow them to bear weight on it'. And then it would be six weeks with my leg in full plaster, no bearing weight on it, before I'd go back in and hope this operation had done some good. This was on and on and on. It was incredibly frustrating.

It caused problems in the family. My sister always felt neglected because I was getting the attention, even though I was just ensconced in the house basically doing nothing. Being a burden, as I saw it. And then obviously it was very frustrating for me on a physical level as well. I was a very sporty kid. I was built to motor on. Everybody remembers me as this like little Duracell bunny that was just always, always going. I was going from crack of dawn to late at night. Fiona would be buzzing along. And then I lost that, was in and out of hospital, on crutches.

Compounding everything, my dad was on strike. My dad was in the mining industry, and the mining industry in the UK was being shut down. It was deemed not profitable. I remember the day it started. My sister had gone for an interview, for medical school. She wanted to be a doctor. My mum was with her, and I was at home waiting for an ambulance to come and take me to physio. And Dad came home, and then he was literally home for a year with no money. That was it. There was no money, no benefits, no support. They were setting up soup kitchens. People were losing their homes, their life, everything.

So that was a really difficult time to be basically stuck in the house. Not being able to walk. Waiting for an ambulance to take you to hospital every day. It was a small house, and everybody was living on top of everyone. Constant worry about what was going on. Would we lose our home? And then me very ill. It didn't make for good times.

It was grim. I never went out as a teenager, never. I had no friends because all the girls my age were at school and doing the things that you grow up as a girl doing. They were getting into boys and whatever, going out to discos. Never any of that for me. It was just Fiona in the house. I couldn't go anywhere, I couldn't do anything.

Mum was doing shift work, and before that she was teaching piano in the house. In the evening pupils used to come and I would have to knock on the door of the front room if I wanted to speak to her. And my sister was off doing her own things. I was pretty much alone, and there wasn't a lot to do. This was well before the time of social media, so it wasn't as if I could Facebook my mates while I was at home. I read quite a lot of books. Apart from that I was very much on my own.

Then I went in to the hospital one day, expecting the same kind of thing, what had become routine, and a new doctor said, 'Look, we've got a serious problem. She needs this kneecap off. This is going to be a big operation and this is going to be very painful. She's probably not going to be able to walk again properly'.

We never truly got an official diagnosis of what the issue was. We were just told there was a massive conglomeration behind my kneecap, it was turning it to jelly, it was crumbling inside and it needed to come out, and it needed to come out quickly. That was the line. We still don't know if that was basically because there'd been so many misdiagnoses previous to that that they wanted to cover up. This was the time before computers, it was handwritten notes, everything was just done in the hospital, written out. You'd just do what the consultant said. You'd go, see your consultant, come away, do what they say, then go back and hope it's going to be all right.

So now we were told the problem was basically a crumbling of the joint, which needed this major corrective surgery and they would have to remove my kneecap.

Shock doesn't really cover it. But we went along with it. I went into hospital, had the operation. And I have to say that I've never been in pain like I was in after that operation. I couldn't lie down. I couldn't move in my bed. I literally couldn't alter my position in my bed. It was the worst pain of my life. But we did think that was going to be it, problem solved. And it probably would have been, but for the fact that when I went to physiotherapy, one of the physiotherapists at the center read my notes wrong.

She thought I'd had a different operation. And I was telling her, 'I literally cannot bend my knee'. So she put me on my stomach and said, 'Yes, you can. You're just not trying'. And she bent my leg back on itself all the way. It was full of internal stitches. I was supposed to do light, gentle exercises. I started screaming.

A guy up the road from us, who was also in the mining industry and therefore on strike, had taken me to the appointment. And when I came home my mum looked at my leg and she was absolutely horrified. It was massive, swollen and awful looking. So my mum went up to see the man who had taken me to the appointment and said, 'John, what the hell have they done to her?' He said, 'Well, I don't know. I just heard her screaming and I brought her home'.

I suppose nowadays it would be considered gross medical negligence and you would be going for some massive compensation claim. But the problem was that my mum was a student nurse at the time. She went to this medical centre and told them she was complaining, that she wanted to see someone, wanted to know what had happened. And they basically said to her, 'If you make a big thing of it, you'll lose your job. There's nothing you can do'. It was a big cover-up, and of course my mum was frightened. Hers was the only wage in the house, my dad was on strike.

We thought it would heal, we thought we could work through it. But it was nearly two years extra healing, and I couldn't really bend it. It got infected, I had all sorts of problems. In the end a family friend stepped in, and I got private medical treatment. It was as sorted out as it was going to get.

To be honest I think that's probably the most pivotal thing in my life, Stanley, the family friend, stepping in, because my parents couldn't do very much. They didn't have the finance, they didn't have the money to be able to help me.

Stanley did. He was a businessman in Chesterfield and he decided that it was going to be his project to fix this problem. He's one of the reasons that I am the person that I am.

To give an example, during this period I had to go to physiotherapy appointments every day. During the week there would be an appointment a day. And my dad wouldn't take me. So this is when Stanley stepped in and offered to help. He said 'I could make myself available. I could take her to the hospital. I could do things for her'.

Another area Stanley helped me with was education. A major consequence of this problem with my knee was that I was not able to go to school. I'd missed out on this whole chunk of schooling because of my leg. There wasn't even any home tutoring offered. I was doing my O levels, and I was fifteen, quite young to be doing my O levels, because my birthday is in August so I was always about a year behind the rest of my class. But I'd been at home so long, I'd missed out on so much schooling, I'd just kind of forgotten at this point. I don't think the school knew what to do, and I certainly didn't.

I remember getting some revise books and looking at them and thinking *Oh my lord, I've got to go and do this exam and I'm just going to be twiddling my thumbs.* I had to have special letters to the exam board to say that if this person needs to get up and move around in the exam, she can do so. She's got an exception to go outside. She needs longer for the exams because she can't sit properly.

I did eventually get my O levels, but it wasn't easy for me. And after that I didn't really know what to do. I was probably about eighteen at the time, but the question was how was I to get a good job to support myself without a good education? That's when Stanley stepped in and paid for private education for me, a private college in Oxford. That's when I moved away from Chesterfield. After that I came to London and worked. If Stanley hadn't helped, I don't where I'd be or what I'd be doing.

I was going to be registered disabled at one point because it looked so hopeless. But we didn't want that and it didn't happen. I never thought that that was going to be me. I was not disabled, I'd had a lot of surgery, but I could get better from that, I'd still got my knee, just not my kneecap.

Though at one point, they didn't know what to do to fasten everything together apparently, and they actually just thought the best and easiest option would be to fuse it so I'd have a straight leg. Mum said 'Absolutely not. That's not going to happen. We know that her knee joint is crumbled, we know we've got problems but that surely can't be the answer'.

Even with all the work that was done on my knee, living with it is an ongoing issue. A few years ago I had a problem with my knee, and I figured *Oh, this is painful. What do I do? I better go to a sports doctor.* So I got myself off to a sports doctor at a hospital in Chelmsford, I trundle in there and I say 'I've got a problem with this knee, but I should explain that I've got no kneecap and I need to know whether you think it's up to doing a marathon'. He said 'Well, if you've been doing these marathons you must have a kneecap'. Because apparently the kneecap is a pivotal fulcrum and you shouldn't be able to run properly without it.

Then I sat there and, stupidly, I started to doubt myself—because I have to say, those teenage years were not pleasant for me and I've got this idea that the only way to get through things is put them in some compartment in my brain where I don't visit very often, and now who was to say I'm remembering correctly? So then I'm sitting in front of him, this young doctor, and I said 'I don't think I've got a kneecap... well, I was told I hadn't got one'. Then I had to call my mum and ask her 'Hey, have I got a kneecap?' and she of course said 'No, you haven't!'

So the doctor said 'Look, let's just get to the bottom of this. I'm going to do this ultrasound on you for free, and then we can find out whether you've got a kneecap or not. Because I've seen you running, and I honestly cannot believe that you can do it without a kneecap'.

So then it's getting really embarrassing. Internally I'm thinking *I hope I've not been going around telling people I haven't got a kneecap when I have*

got one in there, or there's a little one in there, like a mini-kneecap that I didn't know about. Imagine.

He did the ultrasound, and thank heavens, he said, 'No, you haven't got a kneecap'. But he was stunned. He said he couldn't believe that I regularly run marathons, that I do anything athletic, actually, without a kneecap, which he would consider absolutely essential for athletic excellence.

I was just grateful I wasn't completely barmy and going around telling people I hadn't got a kneecap when I did.

People don't believe I can do what I do without it. But they can see it if it's pointed out to them. If anybody sees me run, they say they can see that I flick my leg out on one side. There are real weird things that I still have to think about doing, and one of those things is walking down stairs one at a time. I can do it, but I have to think about doing it, because all those formative years it was one foot down, one foot down, lower myself down with my left leg because I couldn't rely on my right leg. I got into that habit, and I still have to think about how to navigate stairs.

When I came to London a guy at my gym who was a really great coach said 'You can do all sorts of things, but you just look ridiculous when it comes to the stairs'. He said, 'If there's one thing I'm going leave as a legacy in this world, it's going to be teaching you to not keep shuffling about like that'.

It's my big Achilles heel. I've got to shuffle. But he taught me that I could actually walk down stairs properly, and we did all this plyometric stuff that I'd never done before. Before that I did struggle, and even now if I'm tired I have to consciously think, 'Walk down the stairs properly, Fiona. Get a grip'.

I was on and off crutches for four or five years. And even when I came to London, I had to bring my crutches, in case I had some need for them.

I did use a wheelchair for a bit, but that was something I never felt comfortable with, because even though I'd got this problem with my legs—and it was a problem, it was a helluva problem—I felt that I'd got strong arms and I wanted to get about under my own steam as much as possible. And even though they are crutches and you're swinging your leg and you're relying on your arms, I did feel that there was more freedom in that. I hated it when they used to wheelchair me around the hospital.

So that was my childhood. There were good moments obviously, but a lot of circumstances didn't make it blissful, let's put it like that. I don't look back at this time. I don't like revisiting it, I'll be honest, I really do find it difficult. But I'm not bitter. So many people have so much worse. But it has given me, probably, a different perspective on things, a different perspective on life. It was difficult and there were some extraordinarily miserable times, but they've made me the person that I am. I acknowledge them and embrace them for that.

One of the things that I enjoy most is my freedom, being able to decide to go and do something, and decide on my own terms, under my own steam, to go and do something. That's very important to me. It gives me the ability to change my mindset when I'm running.

Sometimes I'm out trudging about for hours on end and I'm thinking *Why am I doing this? This is just awful.* And then you kind of apply reverse psychology. *Yes, it is awful, but think how awful it would be if you couldn't do this. Think how awful it would be for instance if you were sick in a bed and you couldn't do this. At least you've got the ability, the option to decide.* And therefore I feel that that's a blessing.

Or I'm running through a muddy field and I think *Yeah, you're running through a field and it's muddy. But are there any landmines here? No. Well what you moaning about then? Look how blessed you are, look at what some*

16

people are having to live with in war-torn countries. Or if it's really grim and lonely—and it can be bleak where I run—and I'm alone and I'm pushing myself hard, because I have to in order to get myself ready for races, then I think *But hang about, you're moaning because it's so quiet. Think of people in Syria, the bombing that they're facing. And the noises and the screams they're facing. How much would they like just peace and quiet? Or in a slaughterhouse or in places that farm animals, the squealing of animals, the cries. How much would they welcome peace and quiet?*

It's about giving myself a different way of looking at things, so I don't think what I've been through is the worst thing in the world.

I've got a blooming great scar up on my leg, I've got this appalling-looking modge going on. The funny thing is people don't talk about it very much, probably because they're afraid of being rude. The ones that do ask about it though, they'll ask me 'Do you ever think about it when you're running?'

Do I ever think about it when I'm running?

There's a saying, 'Never stand on the start line of a marathon knowing you're carrying an injury'. And I've never stood on the start line of a marathon knowing that I'm not carrying an injury. I'm always carrying one. So I tend to just block it, shove it to the back of my mind. I've stood on elite starts with some prodigiously talented athletes, and as far as I'm concerned I'm doing it as an equal. Even though my body's not equal, I'm not going to make excuses. It's just part of me. And that's it.

Even now, in our household all you'll ever hear if my parents see me do anything is 'Watch your knee. Watch your knee'. That was always the favorite phrase at home. 'Watch what you're doing with that knee. Don't do anything. Watch your knee'. I can't do things like bend it below 90 degrees, I can't kneel down very well. I've got to be very careful.

That's why basically if I was going to run, it was going to be on the road, flat, a straightforward out and back exercise, 26.2 miles in a marathon. When it came to things like the North Pole Marathon or Marathon de Sables—it was out of the question. I never thought I'd be able to do that sort of thing—it never entered my mind I would be able to walk on those extreme terrains, in those extreme conditions, much less run.

In fact, I think it's a security blanket that I tend to run in long leggings, skintight, just to keep my knee supported—or keep me aware that there's some support around it. Because it is tremendously difficult to keep my right leg up to the same strength level as my left leg, and if it fails, then I'm more likely to fall, more likely to get injured and put myself out of running entirely for a period. I've been really, really lucky in that respect. I'm blessed in terms of the fact that apart from the left knee, which I do watch, I have been amazingly resilient with the running.

CHAPTER 4

Cycling and the Sanctuary

COLLEGE WAS WHEN I GOT into cycling, in a sport kind of way—I'd cycled previously when I was much younger. But bikes were the natural form of transport in Oxford. One day I was going home from college on my 'sit up and beg', as we called them, just a regular old thing, and I met a guy who was out on his racing bike. He was on his racing bike in his club clothing and I was on my sit up and beg in a skirt, but I was actually keeping up with him. He said 'Why don't you come down the cycling club?' So I went down there and started to race my bikes again.

Bike racing wasn't easy for me, my leg strength was weak, but a physio had told me that if I could make that turning leg motion that would be ideal for my knee condition because it is not going to cause any instability of the joint, it's just one continuous motion that should be leg strengthening if it's done properly.

So then I went off to the club, and it's very quick with me, one minute you're an amateur, the next minute you're winning races. And that's how it was with me with the bike. I was always out training, I used to ride about four or five hundred miles a week. That's how I started again with the bike racing. I've no talent for any particular sport. I've got a few sports that I'm not too bad at—I was no shoddy rower, I got into rowing when I was in Oxford because Oxford is the place for rowing. I'm just one of those body types that's going to take to certain sports. I'm built for it. I'm short, I'm fairly compact, I'm quite muscular. That's basically it. I just took to bike riding because it was something that I thought I could do and do quite well.

I started on the road, what they call testing and time trialing and road racing. At the time women's cycling was not what it is now. As a woman, you had what they call third cap mens' races, and I remember one of my biggest victories was beating Bradley Wiggins. It's one of my claims to fame, I beat Bradley Wiggins in a race. Granted, he was only about thirteen at the time, but I did beat him.

But I was trying to combine the bike racing with a career. I came to London and I was working and my local velodrome was Harlow. It wasn't ideal. Now they've got Manchester, they've got a whole village there where track riders can go and live on site and be near a track and other track riders. It wasn't like that when I was racing. You were having to do track sessions in the evenings after work and the tracks weren't open all the time. And I'd say that women's cycling hasn't got the profile that it should have today, but it certainly didn't have anything like it does today back then.

There were a number of reasons I stopped bike racing. Number one was it's expensive. Obviously you need a bike—really you need multiple bikes, and you need a lot of other equipment besides. There weren't sponsors out there, there was no exposure for women's racing, so you had to try to cover everything yourself. And the one thing that never did sit pretty with me with the bike racing is the drugs that are involved in it. I never felt comfortable being around that kind of environment and the pressure that's put on you to toe the line with that. That pressure is there and has always been there, especially with the male coaches.

So when I met my partner Martin in London, I was heavily into my racing my bikes, but I was also working as a temp at the place Martin was working at. The way we got involved was because at the time I had a couple of pit bulls and loads of small animals that I'd rescued ad hoc, and I was in this rented accommodation where I really shouldn't have had animals of any sort. And then my landlord said she wanted to sell the property and I'd have to get out. So she gave me notice and I was left to figure out what to do with all these animals and all these bikes that I'd accumulated for track and road and time trialing and whatnot.

I thought the solution would be to buy a place somewhere, which would have been out of the question for me except that my family very kindly gave me the deposit, so I was going to buy a house where I could have the animals. I wanted to get this place with a big enough backyard that I could have my pony, Max, move down from Chesterfield to live with me in London. The unfortunate thing was that the house didn't become available to buy before I had to leave the rented accommodation.

At the time I was working in London for this guy who was terribly posh, at a finance place. My boss's mother or grandmother or something was lady in waiting to the Queen, and he lived in Wimbledon with his wife and their three children. He told me 'Look, Fiona, you work for me, I feel responsible for you, you haven't got anywhere to live in essence, you'll have to come and live with me'. I told him that was a really kind offer, but I didn't think that Wimbledon and his wife and all would take to me in the same way, especially not when I come with this giant menagerie of animals and bikes and goodness knows what. So he said he took my point but he still felt responsible for me, and he had an idea. And he marched me round to the desk Martin was sitting at and said 'Martin, you know Fiona, she works for me', 'Yeah, yeah', 'You live in Ongar, where Fiona's going to buy her house?' And Martin says he does, and my boss goes 'Okay then, well Fiona will have to come and move in with you'.

So one Sunday morning, after I'd been to a race and I'd won my race and I got a big bouquet of flowers, I just turned up on his doorstep. I think it was Easter time, because I remember his parents had just come and they were standing there with a palm cross, they'd just been to church. And I turned up with all these bikes, and I'd got this skin-suit on with a joker and a little devil on my sandal and I remember his mother just looking at me like 'What the heck is that? What are you doing?' I must have looked like an alien or something to her.

So I moved in with him and then I just kind of never moved out. Because Martin, he wasn't into animals the way I was, but we just clicked.

Shortly after that is when we got the sanctuary. One of the horses that I got rescued at a livery yard, Oscar, had a terrible accident and he nearly lost his life. He was at the vet for 13 weeks and that was when we decided we couldn't keep on with it. We had animals everywhere, we were paying £800 a week to various livery yards and farms to keep these horses, and they weren't doing it the way I wanted it done. They weren't looking after them, weren't respecting them, the other people down there were always bickering—it wasn't a peaceful and tranquil environment for them to be in.

It was causing a lot of problems. I used to have to go and see to the horses before I went to work, then I had a 30-mile cycle into work, then I had a full day's work to do. I was in one of those jobs where sometimes I was working 36 hours through. Merchant banking. Then I'd cycle home and see to the horses—it was incredibly difficult, and we were paying a lot of money for the horses to be kept. So we decided the only thing to do was to try to buy a place with land somewhere. Which was absolutely incomprehensible to me, a complete dream. I never ever thought it would be a reality.

I thought the only way to afford the kind of upgrade in property we were talking about, especially near London, was to come from some kind of massively monied family. One of us at least needed to keep working. The sanctuary was funded by us mainly. So we found this place that was about three times as expensive Martin's house was worth, and I remember when I first saw the literature on it I just put it in the bin. I thought *It's too dear, put it in the bin.*

But somehow we eventually did get the money together. A lot of it was down to my mum and my family. Two days before Oscar came back from the vet, after being there 13 weeks, we took delivery of Tower Hill Stables, our animal sanctuary.

Because we were so tight on money—I mean for the first year or two we were here we had nothing—and my job then was going to be care for the animals full time and look after the place, it just wasn't viable to keep on with my cycling. It's expensive, it's high maintenance, and not just financially. If you want to be a decent bike rider you've got to really go out in a group. I used to go out in a group with Matt Illingworth and Rob Hayles, who won an Olympic silver medal on a pursuit. You have to be in that competitive environment cranking it up and you've got to have the bikes, you've got to have the equipment, you have to spend a lot money. So we decided that I wouldn't do that anymore and I sold my bikes, to help get the money together for the sanctuary.

Then I just settled in to looking after the animals. That didn't last too long though. I was thinking to myself more and more as the sanctuary grew that yes, for sure we were taking in rescued cattle, we could take

23

in pigs, I could just say yes to all the types of animals that I'd had to say no to in the past. It wasn't enough though, because I knew I could take in 400 or 4,000 or 4,000,000 animals, but it's not going to stop the real problem. The real problem is the way the animals are treated and exploited within the food chain. That's what I really wanted to address, but I didn't think there was anything I could do about that. But I wanted to keep fit, so that's when I took up jogging, and then I realised I was pretty good at running.

I didn't realise how good until I entered a race, a half marathon, and I won it—broke the course record, in fact. That's when I thought *This isn't just a keep fit thing anymore.* This is something that I probably could use to benefit the promotion of veganism through sport. And that's when I asked myself, *What's probably the most difficult event you can do running?* I knew I wasn't that fast and was never going to be that fast. At the time I thought the ultimate challenge was marathon running. So I thought, *Okay, I'll just see how good I can be at running a marathon.* I thought that would have to lay all the doubters and naysayers to bed, because if I could do well in a marathon, then it would prove that a long-term vegan diet is not prohibitive to doing well in extreme sport.

CHAPTER 5

The Start of a Marathon

THIS IS WHEN THE MARATHON running kicked in. There was no great desire behind it, it was just something physically that I thought I could make work for the animals. The other reason I chose running is it's cheap to do, it's flexible, you can do it any time day or night, and you don't need a lot of equipment.

But it's a funny story with the running. I don't like running, particularly. I like being free, I like to go out and be in the environment. That's great. But when you start putting pressure on yourself—'I need to run that time on that day on that morning in four months' time', and there's a lot depending on it, it doesn't feel so free.

I am trying to do something positive with my running. I'm not just out eying up a trophy, or thinking that I need to get my time down. I am doing this with a reason, and it isn't anything like personal gratification. But when you're doing this for others, you then start putting a lot of pressure on yourself and you start to think 'Yes, but if I could top 20 in a race, or I could top 10 in the biggest race in the world, then I could make an extra impact'. So you're training very, very hard, and anyone will tell you that when you're in that zone of hard, pressurised training, it's not that pleasant. These aren't fun runs. You might do two sessions in a day and three sessions of speed work every week, and you might do an easy six, eight mile recovery run in the evening. But even though that's at an easy pace, it's not actually easy, because you've done the speed session that morning, and you've got a long run to do the following day. Everything you're doing is fatiguing, you're trying to get the maximum out of every session. So there isn't anything easy in there.

When I figured out that I'm not too bad at this running thing, I looked for a coach to give me some guidance. At the time it wasn't like you could go 'Oh, I'll just Google "How to run a quick marathon" and then maybe watch a YouTube tutorial or find a training guide on the internet'. There wasn't any of that. So I thought *Okay, I'm getting some good results here, I'll find a coach who can take me to that next level.* I've always put a lot of pressure on myself to achieve big things with running, to draw attention to the animals.

But I couldn't find anyone to take me on. Everyone I asked said yes, you've got some ability, but I'm not going to invest my time in you because you're not going to take my advice. You might take it with the training, but I don't think you'll be able to get the best out of yourself because of your diet.

So I've always trained alone, and consequently I am very amateur in what I do regarding my running. I do it with a professional dedication, but I don't really know that much about running. And to tell the truth I don't really care that much about running. I just care about the results I can get from the running. People who are familiar with my results think that I'm going to be some sort of expert, but all I can tell them is what I have done, which may very well not be the best methods.

All my time is taken up here at the sanctuary, seven days a week. If I'm not off on a run, I am at the sanctuary. So when I go off to run, it's got to be worth running. And I don't want bags full of medals and little wins. I don't want that. I want to get the best out of myself for the most economical financial and time investment that I can. Because I've taken up running with a very specific reason, I've looked at it very honestly and asked myself why would I want to go and run some small race every week? It's time-consuming, it's not that productive. There's not going to be the publicity gain that I want from it for the animals, for veganism, for the positivity. It's going to be added expense. It's just not worth it.

So I looked at it and thought yes, it's all very well going and doing well in local races, but that's not going to get me the exposure I want. So I've raced very, very lightly. In the first part of my running career, I focused on two races a year only. That would be two marathons. A spring and an autumn race. I never did anything in between, apart from train for them. I think that's helped me keep injury-free, because I haven't continually done that high impact pounding over and over again, or over-raced. I've just worked out a schedule that I know I can maintain over a training block and stuck to it. I think that's actually made my body more physically able to cope. Because I do think people can be tempted to over-race.

To me, you can only race—what I would actually call race, which is running for your best—in a few events a year. You can't go week in, week out, and just keep churning out the same old, same old, especially the longer distances. You've got to be specifically targeting one or two or three races. And that's what I've always done.

It hasn't been easy. I've got no coach, nobody to tell me what to do or what not to do. I train alone all the time. I have to truly believe that whatever effort I'm putting in on any given day, on race day there's going to be a reward for it. I'm short of time, it's horrible weather, and I'm tired. But I've got to believe that by going out and doing that run, that training, it is going to make a difference on that race day somewhere in the future.

That belief has been one of my greatest strengths, and underlying that belief is the motivation that allows me to do it all. I am not doing it for myself. I don't want anything for myself that badly that would drive me that hard and make me that determined.

I'm not in any way comparing myself to the great Haile Gebrselassie, but I remember I was invited to go to the Amsterdam Marathon in 2005 by the race organisers, and in the race hotel on the Friday before the race on Sunday, Haile spent some time with me and we chatted about why he does what he's does. He was going for a world record, and he talked about a few things that I recognised from my own approach. He didn't particularly enjoy the training. He enjoyed the results that the level of training that he did at the time brought. And a lot of his motivation was the people of Ethiopia. I think at one point someone told me that about 10,000 people's livelihoods depended on him doing well in races, that he could earn money and recognition, that he could employ people in Ethiopia.

I drew a lot of inspiration from that, because before that I'd thought all these other athletes, they must love it. They must be out there training and enjoying it and thinking it's great. And they don't. It's a lot of hard effort at the top and there isn't any easy way I've found to do it. Because I lack talent, and I lack ability. But the strength I've got is that I recognise that. So I'm willing to work with what I've got rather than believing I've got more than I have. And I believe in myself.

I've always felt quite embarrassed when I'm invited to these mega races and people are looking at me thinking, 'And you are … ?' A 'What are you doing here?' kind of thing. I know I don't look the same as everybody else, I mean the other elite women, they're really talented and they've got coaches and advisors and you go to technical meetings and they're all discussing their race plans—and my plan is just basically to get from A to B as quickly as I can without dying in between. I haven't got a plan beyond that.

I'm not thinking, *Okay, I'll get to 20K and open my pace*, because to me when you're running a marathon, basically you're racing yourself, and that's it. You want to do your best, you want to get the absolute best out of yourself on the day and make sure there's nothing left in the barrel—but you don't want to overdo it, you don't want to go into debt. So I'm honest about it. I am not that brilliant a runner, I'm not that quick a runner, but I am willing to work with the little advantages that I have got, such as being fairly strong and very motivated. And I've got a will of iron. But other than that, I don't have much ego involved—I'm not that into flattery or the trappings that can come with good results. I've got a few trophies and medals and suchlike, but not a lot. I've not got loads of pictures of myself. I've done my races for the promotion of what I believe in. Once I've done the job, I just come home and get on with what I think of as the real me, and real life, which is looking after the animals.

So I do brush things aside a bit, and some people think it's false modesty, or me being cavalier about it, but I'm not—it's that I'm a 'job done, let's get on to the next job' person. I can honestly say in all that I've ever done, I've never been particularity satisfied with anything. Yes, I've thought, *That was pretty good*, but it's always followed by *How could I have made it that bit better?* or *What could I have done to challenge myself a bit more?* or *Would this or that have made a difference in training?* I don't rest

29

on my laurels; I don't crave praise. Probably because in terms of what I'm trying to achieve in the promotion of veganism, my results never seemed to get the result that I wanted.

When I tell people I've got 8th place in the Amsterdam Marathon or top twenty in London and Berlin and the Great North Run—and these are the biggest races in the world, these are not for messing around with—people are flabbergasted. A guy that I know from the local running club, I remember once, I was in the London Marathon, and I was running with an extremely good female runner from London—very talented, very quick. And this guy saw me running with her and when it'd gone to the results page he'd assumed that she would beat me. And he looked for my result and he couldn't find me because he was looking behind her time and he said, 'It never even occurred to me you beat her by that much'. That didn't particularly hurt me, because I thought, *Well, yeah, I can see that, that you probably wouldn't think that I would beat such a good runner.*

People are genuinely shocked when they know the times I've run and the places I've got. People don't really expect me to be as quick as I am. Sometimes I have to joke and say 'Yeah, but I know a shortcut' or something like that, and then I can see them think, *Wait, does she?* (No, I don't.)

But it just seems the least I can do, in view of the incomprehensible extent of the problem I'm trying to address. It just seems the least I can do that while I'm walking the planet and I'm able to do it, I should put one hundred percent into what I'm doing. When people say to me, 'Well you say you haven't got the rewards you wanted, but what would you be satisfied with?' The answer isn't that I'm craving a trophy for a first place finish in the London Marathon or anything like that, it's that I haven't got the publicity I wanted for the veganism through the running. I really thought that if you ran top twenty in some of the biggest races in the world, if you ran 2.38 in a marathon, you would at least get somebody to say, 'Wow, that's really quick for an amateur runner who's doing it on a plant-based diet'.

But I wasn't getting press attention or publicity. I'd be spending a lot of energy training 100 miles a week for a 10-week block before a marathon. Dedicating yourself to it, it puts you under a lot of stress and then you come to your tapering period and you're paranoid about getting ill, you're paranoid about getting an injury. It impacts your family life. I've got a niece and I couldn't go to her christening because I was tapering for a race and I was so scared about getting ill or getting a cold from any of the congregation that I couldn't go. People know that on Christmas Day for instance you are not going to be sitting down for a family meal at lunchtime, you're going to be going out training, that's what you do, that's part of you.

You are sacrificing and it does impact your personality because you get very stressed out, you get very worried, very nervous before these events. It feels like you're damned if you do train, and you're damned if you don't. And meanwhile I'm still not achieving what I wanted in terms of publicity. I thought, *Is it something that I'm doing wrong? I'm obviously just not good enough. Have to go and do a bit better in my next race*, and *How do I get to that next level?* I'd gone completely demented, thinking *What do I need to do?* After a while I thought I'm just not good enough, I'll pack up, I don't care. I'm not going to dedicate this amount of energy to something that I don't think will ever really pay off. I'll just look for an alternative. I'm obviously never going to win the London Marathon, that's not going to happen. I'm not going to do any better in these big races than I've been doing in them, and my results are not achieving my goal. So I'll look at switching to winning. See if I can win other races and break course records and see if that achieves what I want to achieve.

CHAPTER 6

Fire Crew

HOW I GOT INVOLVED WITH firefighting is quite simple. In our area we have what's called a retained fire service, and they are retained by the whole time fire brigade to provide cover for the area without literally having a group of firemen sitting in a fire station who are going to be called out very infrequently. However, to get into the retained fire service you have to meet the same physical criteria as a whole time firefighter. In other words, you have to be able to do the identical job, have the identical fitness levels, but you're not doing it as a profession, which is really very limiting in terms of who you can recruit.

So I was out running one day and a car pulled up next to me, the window got wound down and a bloke shouted to me, 'Oi, you', and I thought, *Here we go, what have I done wrong this time?* Expecting to get some abuse or something. He said, 'You look fit, have you ever considered becoming a firefighter?' To which I replied, 'No, it doesn't cross my mind every day, but tell me more'. He said, 'Come down to the fire station in Tillingham tomorrow and I'll tell you'. I thought he was mad because I didn't think there even was a fire station in Tillingham. But I looked, and sure enough, there was.

So I went down the next day and it was all explained to me. Our role is identical to the fire brigade's, but we do it on a part-time basis. We carry an alerter, and if this alerter goes off, within five minutes you must attend the fire station. Day or night, you jump, grab your gear, you get in the fire planes or the pump and you go and do the job of the firemen.

You can only be unavailable for the fire service if you physically go up to the fire station and sign yourself out as unavailable. Otherwise if your alerter goes off in your pocket, you have to go. No matter what you're doing, you drop everything. So if you're in bed asleep and it goes off, you get in your car in your nightdress, you go and you do it.

And I don't know what made me think *Well that sounds like a good idea; how do I do that?* But I asked. And he said I'd have to go through the same full physical fitness criteria that a firefighter does. Obviously it's a very male-dominated domain, at that time especially. That was another one of my veganophobia incidents as well. You have to go to the whole-time fire station in Witham for a physical assessment, to check that you're physically strong enough, that you can run out the hoses and all that. So, I go down there for my physical assessment and it was all going quite to plan, and then we had a break. And during this break the lady from the canteen brought out some cups of tea, in which she put cow's milk. So I said no, not really interested, I'll go without. To which the response was, you can't go without, you'll dehydrate, you need to drink. It's a cold day and you need a hot drink. And I had to blurt it out that because I'm a vegan, I don't drink cow's milk, and oh my lord the kerfuffle. The fireman who was recruiting just came and pushed his face into mine and he said,

'The last one of those we had down here lasted three hours. But that was a man'. And I thought, *Oh Lord, I've got a whole day of this.*

In the end I did really well in that physical assessment, and he did come apologise afterwards. He said, 'I wouldn't have thought you could be that strong, I'm sorry'.

So I passed the physical and written tests and went through the training and became a retained firefighter. It seemed like a good idea because you could be flexible in terms of the fact you had money but you could sign off. So I could make myself available to the fire service at a time when I knew Martin was going to be available for the animals, say between 8 p.m. at night and 8 a.m. in the morning. I could commit to turning up at the fire station if there was a call because I knew that I could leave the sanctuary in safe hands. Same thing at weekends and bank holidays. I could make up the deficit in the manpower that they needed up there without jeopardizing the sanctuary, and I could also earn extra money.

That was basically how I got involved with the firefighting. It wasn't like it was always a great passion of mine, a dream that one day I would become a retained firefighter. It was just something that, again, I knew I could use, and get some extra money for the sanctuary.

At the Tillingham station it's very ad hoc. You can get six shouts in a day when you're in and out, in and out, and then you can have nothing for eight weeks. We get a lot of fuel fires around here. The idea of the retained fire service is to deal with all minor incidents, to keep the whole-time firefighters, who are obviously short on funding, and time, in the city environments. And if the retained firefighters need backup, then that gives the whole-time firefighters time to come and take over, because you're out there addressing an incident. But we're left alone a lot out here; it's a long way to the nearest whole-time station.

We have the mudflats out on the estuary, so you get people getting stuck in the mudflats. We also get a lot of RTAs, road traffic accidents, around here. A lot of situations where you have to cut people out of vehicles after they've had impacts. My first call, I had to crawl in a vehicle and get a man out who'd died at the wheel; he'd had a heart attack. That quite shocked me because I'd never actually had the experience of handling a dead body before that. And then all of a sudden I'm in there with this other firefighter I didn't know very well, trying to grapple this poor elderly gentleman out of his car. It's quite harrowing.

We went to one house fire in a local community and I got told off because I rescued a rabbit and we're not supposed to effect rescues of the pets, but I did.

At another house fire, there was a child in a wardrobe and we crawled in and got the breathing apparatus on the child and got them out, and it was all quite traumatic. And then as we're there in front one resident asked me if I could go back in for his television. The house was in flames—no, we're not going back in for a television! He said, 'But it's brand new and it's 54 inch'. And then we subsequently found out that in the roof of this particular property they've got a load of contraband fireworks just waiting to go off.

It's just another dimension to an already rather bizarre life. But it's given me a lot of skills that I wouldn't necessarily have had. I wouldn't know how to do a lot of the things that I do now, practical things, that the fire service has taught me a lot about that. Rescue equipment, basic medical knowledge, first aid, things like that. So it's had its benefits and bonuses.

We had one incident actually, just as the foot-and-mouth crisis hit this country, if you had cloven-hoofed animals you were absolutely on lockdown, and obviously we've got cloven-hoofed animals. My mum would come down from Chesterfield, where they were living at the time, to stay with me. It was absolutely devastating. You couldn't come in, you couldn't go out, no deliveries unless the animals were hosed down and disinfected. It was terrible.

There was a call at the gate and I went outside and all I remember seeing was this giant woman. I'd never seen a woman this tall, ever. And she was wearing this white suit. She was from the Ministry of Agriculture and Fisheries and Food. At the time, they had to come round and inspect every premise that had cloven-hoofed animals. And she said, 'Nothing to worry about'. Nothing to worry about? She's dressed in a white suit with her wellies on and she looks like she come out of some kind of sci-fi film. She said, 'I just need to see your cattle passports and make sure that you're all registered'. And I just went blank. I think it must have been because I was so shocked, but I couldn't remember where we'd put them. We'd moved the older stuff that was outside into the house, made a little office and Martin had done most of it. And I couldn't remember where the passports were. So I got a great big pile of stuff in my arms and I went out and I said, 'They must be in here somewhere'.

And then at that very minute my fire service alerter went off. My mum was standing there and all she remembers seeing is me drop the stuff in front of this woman and just leg it up the drive into my car. I think the inspector just thought I'd not got the passports for the cows and I'd just run away. My mum explained I was in the fire brigade and I had this alerter and if it's gone off I have to go. The woman asked when I'd be back, and Mum said oh, it could be four or five hours. And like, yeah, right. But fortunately the shout we got went right past the house. So two or three minutes later the we go by, *nee-nee-nee-nee*, and the woman said, 'Ah, right, okay I believe you'.

CHAPTER 7

A Reason for Action

I WANT PEOPLE TO UNDERSTAND why I do what I do, and the heart of that reason is that the situation of animals raised for food, it's just horror from start to finish. I find it really hard to believe, but I think a lot of people must not understand that the products they see in packages in the supermarkets were once living, feeling, sentient creatures. I don't understand that they don't understand that. That's the first problem I've got. But a lot of people categorise animals so the rules don't apply to farm animals. It's okay to do it to a pig because pigs are dirty and smelly. The ignorance I find towards animals in the dairy industry is quite startling. They think that's all right because cows make milk, as if they're milk machines or something.

A cow's milk is designed for her baby. It's not designed for human babies or adults. And why does the calf not get the milk? Because the calf is taken away from the mother and exploited in another way while the mother is exploited to produce these insupportable volumes of milk. And people seem to think that's okay because they have a 'nice life'. I think that's the problem with the whole meat-dairy-farmed animal industry, is that people are led to believe that A) it's okay to exploit animals, but B), almost that they're not being exploited, they're doing it voluntarily, or they don't mind, or that that's what they're bred for so it's okay.

I think part of it is that people don't question it, because they don't want to question it, because they don't want to hear the truth—the truth very often isn't attractive. It's like with the marathon running. If people say oh what's the trick, what's your secret, what do you eat? they think I'm going to go, 'Oh I've got this special little potion here and if you take this you'll run really quickly'. They don't really want to hear I train really hard and it's pretty grim and I do it religiously and it's unforgiving but it gets the results. That's like, Oh, no, no, no. So there's nothing we can buy? No. There's nothing, there's no quick way. They don't want to hear that. And they don't want to hear the truth about the animals in animal agriculture. They just don't want to know for whatever reason.

The animals are exploited from the minute they are born to the moment they die. And I try to refrain from using the words 'life' and 'live', because these animals exist. They don't have a life and they don't live. They have no access to natural instincts, natural environments, natural lifespans, nothing about their life is pleasant and nothing about their life is acceptable in my opinion. It is an existence. A horrid existence. The horror falls on them, but it reflects on us as a human race that we are allowing this to continue.

Farrowing crates, where sows are kept in pens and they aren't even allowed to get up—they're not allowed to have contact, they aren't allowed to have bedding—as humans if we are bad and we do wrong, the worst thing that can be inflicted on us is incarceration. We are put within a prison, we are denied our freedom. Yet we think this is okay for animals on a daily basis just because we want to consume their flesh? It's just so wrong on so many levels. I don't know which level to start at to say it's indefensible. There's no need for it. There's no justification for it.

A lot of people don't seem to relate to birds, to feel that birds are worthy. 'Oh, it's only a bird'. 'I'm vegetarian but I eat chicken and fish'. As if to say they don't actually count. But when you actually look at these factory farms, chickens are crammed together in barns, they never see the light of day, they're pecking each other to death. The growth hormones they must be giving to these birds is absolutely phenomenal. I could show you chickens that we've got down in the stables that are fully grown, they're lean, they're healthy, they've got some flight access. These farmed birds are going from hatching to fully grown, ready-to-slaughter in six to eight weeks. They pump them full of steroids and growth hormones. They are living these horrible unnatural lives. The hens are kept in full daylight with lights all the time so they continue to lay. They have no privacy, they have no access to places where they can be alone, they're just grouped together in barns where they are so frustrated they peck each other or peck themselves. Then they are rounded up, crammed into crates, and then they are driven to slaughterhouses where they are hung upside-down and their throats are cut. That is a hen's existence.

One thing I've learned through keeping animals, and we've got a lot of animals, is there is no viable way financially of keeping an animal through a natural lifespan. You can't do it. It's not financially viable. To provide for them adequately, properly, is very expensive. And so to do it commercially, the corners are cut to such a level where it is completely unacceptable for the animal and only acceptable for the people who are making the profits from it. It's just not possible to do it any other way. There's no way anybody can have any sort of freedom-friendly factory. It's too expensive, it's not viable, and I can't honestly see in the 21st century, why bodies such as the British government continue to prop up animal agriculture to the extent and level they do.

If it was any other industry, it would be closed down. I speak from experience: My father was in the mining industry. It was deemed unviable commercially. It was making a loss. Therefore the pits were closed down. Miners fought for their jobs and they went on strike. The decision came down to whether the industry was commercially viable or not. No, so we closed it down. Yet we continue to offer subsidies to the farming industry to keep producing meat and dairy products. And to me, that is unjustifiable on any level. Whether you're looking at it from pure animal ethics, the environment, human health—it's just ridiculous. It's unsustainable and unless something gives, and in my opinion gives very soon, it's going to implode in a horrible global mess of climate change and health problems. I can't think of any way of justifying it. I've tried to get my head around it so many times and there's no way, I can't understand what is driving it.

CHAPTER 8

Freedom to Run

I SOMETIMES FEEL EMBARRASSED when I say that what drives me on is the suffering of animals in the factory farming industries and the cruelty that's going on in the world today. For example, take the Marathon des Sables: It is a tough race, it's a brutal race. Indescribably hot. Never goes below about 50 degrees. You've got sandstorms, you've got a marathon to do a day, one day you've got an 80K, you've got jebels to climb, you've got sand to deal with, you've got all sorts of problems. But I say I feel embarrassed because the caveat to all this is that at any point I can put my hand up and say, 'Actually I've had enough and I want to go home now'. You can. The animals can't. So it's just a drop in the ocean, what I'm doing. I'm putting myself through it, and obviously because I'm doing it for a purpose, failing is a disaster for me. It's not something I've got written on my agenda, that I'm going to fail. But even so, I always know

41

that at any point I can make it stop. Therefore I can't truly say what it must feel like when this isn't an option, this is your life.

When I did MDS in 2012, I was with a group of people who were pretty well-to-do. They came from affluent backgrounds and we turned up, we get in this tent, and there was a lot of moaning going on. 'Where are the Egyptian cotton sheets?' and 'This is about as horrendous as it gets' and we were living 'like tramps'. It wasn't pretty. And by the long stage— the ones of us that made it through the long stage—they'd completely changed their attitude. We dragged the carpet out of the tent and lay there in the sun and we're all there in our filth and we've got no food and we look dreadful. And people were saying 'This is about as good as it gets, isn't it? We can stop, no running to do for the next few hours and it's warm and we've got through the long stage.' And that is how your mindset transfers from 'this is horrendous' to you realizing that these are the only bits and pieces that matter. Everything becomes so precious.

Everyone asks what you do in MDS when you finish each stage. And there's all these exciting things to do, like getting back to your tent and counting your painkillers and working out how many boiled sweets you're going to have the next day—some riveting stuff that goes on. But the point I'm trying to make is that for that short period of time, this is your world and these are your worldly possessions and there have been times where if somebody were to offer me a 500 euro note I'd think, *Well the best I could do is probably blow my nose with it*—that's about the most use it's got when you're stuck out there. And if somebody were to offer you a gold bar you'd say no thank you, because you wouldn't want to have to carry it in your bag, thanks very much.

So you realise that these things that people value so highly outside of this environment are very superficial. Out there everything you have is very precious. And then if you can go into these races, and very few people can, they come away and many think *Oh, I did it, I can brag about that*, but if you actually go in and allow it to change your life you can then look at the news and what's happening in places with wars and disasters in a completely different light. You can realise how truly blessed you are to turn your tap on and have water come out. To not be frightened for your life on a daily basis. To not be worried where you put your feet because you might tread on a landmine—you really do feel blessed for these things. And then when you see these images on the telly, it's not just some soap opera that's in the corner of your room and when you turn that off it goes away. It doesn't go away for those people and it doesn't go away for those animals, that suffering never goes away.

You can make it stop, you can pull out of your race, you can turn your telly off, but it's never stopping for them. It's a 24/7 horror scenario. And I'm not saying you have to live with that every minute of your day and night, because if you do it just turns you into an angry person whose anger becomes so great it becomes unproductive and you implode on yourself. I used to be that person. What changed was I decided the anger was either going to kill me, or I was going to channel that anger into doing something positive.

And that's what I've tried to do with every aspect of my life. Whether it's looking after 600 animals or whether it's running a marathon at the North Pole. It's simply trying to take that angst and make it into something positive that's going to benefit others. Always realizing that whatever I do, in the scheme of things, whether it be in the number of animals that I can save or the amount of people I can reach, it's the best I can do. I want to use every experience very honestly, and always keep them with me. I'm not one of those people that walks away and thinks, *Hmm, got away with that.* I will learn the lessons. And I always want to continue learning. I'm not perfect, I've made mistakes, I've done things that are wrong, I've

43

done things that I would do better next time. But as long as you learn from them, then that's what keeps moving you forward, I believe. That's what keeps moving me forward.

I like caring for the animals, that's what I do. I don't want to hand it off to someone else, I want to do it myself. And when we took the sanctuary on, I always wanted it to be a home, not just a place where animals could be cared for; and I suppose that's where my problem lies. Even if I employed another person to do it, one person wouldn't or couldn't do it. The only reason that I can do it is because I know the animals, and I know their behavioural patterns so well, that I can kind of preempt problems that other people probably couldn't see. And while I can do that I want to do it, because I know that by me doing this full-on amount of work, I can do so much more, and have so many more animals than I could if I was getting someone else to do it.

My parents have moved in because we simply can't pay off the mortgage. When we moved in here we had a big mortgage, and we've kept extending it because of the sanctuary. So it went on and on, and on and on, and now it's coming to the point when the building society wants money back, we've got no money. Spent it all on the animals. My parents, they used to live in Derbyshire, then they moved from Chesterfield down to Tillingham, the village that I run through. My mum is brilliant anyway, she does a lot of cooking and cleaning, everything for the sanctuary, so the idea was that they moved in with us and help to pay the mortgage off, because otherwise it ain't going to happen.

Every penny we've got has always gone into the sanctuary, absolutely everything we've got. My mum's too. When we were trying to buy the sanctuary, she sold her engagement ring, a piano—everything had to go. That's how it's been ever since we've been here.

44

Up until recently the house was just a no-go zone. There were points when we had 22 dogs in the house, and of course I'm here alone while Martin's at work, so if I'm out running or I'm outside, the dogs are just doing what dogs do all over the house.

People ask what sort of animals we take in. Let me tell you, people don't ask you to take in young, healthy, fit, well-trained dogs. And people don't come to you and say, 'I'm really looking for something elderly, something on expensive medication, and preferably we'd like it to be incontinent'. They're not going to come to you for that. We get the ones they're getting rid of. Animal rescue goes in cycles. Whatever the latest celebrity trend is, a few years down the line you will end up with that breed or type of animal. So if it's pot-bellied pigs, if it's Dalmatians, if it's German Shepherds, pygmy goats—you're going to get a flurry of people buying them irresponsibly and then a few years down the line breeding them just as irresponsibly, and then that's when you're going to get them flooding into your sanctuary.

So we had a lot of elderly breed type dogs in the house. They chewed everything. They chewed the doorframes; the carpets were just gone. So when my parents said, 'We'll move down there', it was impossible. It was not habitable. That's when the work had to start to actually make it so that four people instead of two could live in that property. All the furniture, the décor and everything in there has come from my parents' house, because prior to them moving in the dogs had just gone through systematically and ruined every single thing that we had, everything. You just learn to let it go.

You learn to detach yourself from those kind of material things, and just think, *Okay, that's the way it is. A life is much more important than a shoe*—or whatever they've had hold of, the latest thing. People have asked

45

me if I regret it. The answer is no, because at the end of day the house is just bricks and mortar. And even though the house is nice now, and it's all done, it doesn't turn me; I am just so used to not having it, I don't actually want it anymore.

Some people, when they get back from a long run, go and take a hot shower and concentrate on recovering. That's not what I do. I come back from a run and next thing I'm out in the yard mucking out the stables and caring for the animals. The animals always come first, and the running is just a secondary job.

So sometimes when people ask me to recall races and things like that it's almost like asking me to remember something that I was doing for the animals like eight or nine years ago, something very mundane. It's just been a physical action that I've gone through to get those results. So I don't fixate on it at all. I can remember animals and people and details about them because they're the important things to me. The running and collecting trophies and medals, that's not important to me. It's not been the reason I've done it.

CHAPTER 9

Vegan Runner

My first marathon was the Brentwood Half Marathon, and I really can't tell you how little I knew. I just turned up, stood there, set off and ran, and just happened to run quicker than everyone else. It was sort of surreal, because I was coming from this lone, amateur running. I'd never even run next to anyone before that race. I'd only been out alone on the roads. There were some quite serious runners. It was back in a time before marathons and half marathons became quite so commercial, so, generally speaking, people who were doing them were doing them because they actually were into running, rather than any alternative reason like keeping fit as the main motivator.

So my first race, I turned up and won it, and it was quite a shock. That's when I thought, *Oh, I can run a half marathon. It's only 13 miles. Perhaps I could run a marathon*, which is the definitive test—or it was at the time—of ultra-endurance.

It was just identifying something that was hard, still is to this day. It's still a go-to when people talk about significant athletic accomplishments, 'Oh, I'd like to run a marathon'. But I didn't want to get round a marathon, that to me isn't running a marathon. Running a marathon is actually getting out there and going at the fastest pace you can maintain in the race. Just *completing* it wasn't really on the agenda. It was doing the best that I possibly could for the animals. So it wasn't about just running a marathon, it was about doing really, really well in races. Otherwise I didn't want to dedicate my time to it.

That's when I decided to enter an actual race and see how I got on in it. I entered the Moscow Marathon, which probably begs the question, 'Why did you choose the Moscow Marathon?' The answer is basically that I just wanted to go over there. I'd heard about the difficulties they were having with animal issues after *perestroika*, and I wanted to go out there and see for myself what it was like. I don't really know, I act from the heart, I wanted to go. I felt that I wanted to go and do this race. There weren't that many marathons around at the time. Marathons have now sprung up everywhere. Everywhere has now got a marathon, but at the time they didn't. So off I went to Moscow and ran in that marathon.

I have to say that when people ask me which country in the world was most receptive towards veganism, they are absolutely poleaxed when I say, definitely, without a shadow of a doubt, Russia. They were so excited to have a vegan there. They didn't even dumb it down.

I am very heavily involved with Russia. I've got a sanctuary out there, and I've done a lot of work out in Russia to promote animal rights and welfare issues. The Asian leg of the world record that I did, I figured I could probably go to Russia and do it there, and I did. I went to Omsk, and it was just absolutely awesome.

When I was going onto the podium to collect my medal, someone was translating the commentary for me, and they were telling me that, 'There's this amazing woman coming on next, and she's a really strong and positive role model for everybody here', and I'm thinking, 'Oh who is she? Where is she?' and then it turned out it was me. They called me up on stage, and my first thought was, *Blimey, if they think you're tough in Siberia, you really must be tough.* It was also quite humbling how much they didn't shy away from the fact that I'm vegan. The translator told me that they were emphasizing the fact that this person is doing this for a reason, she's doing it for the world records and they were appreciative of me being there.

It was really amazing. They had TV crews out there. They'd got kids lining the streets with little banners of Percy Bear. They were tremendously positive towards the whole thing. So I returned home from that race on a bit of a high.

My entire career has been like that, unformulated. It just kind of fell into place. It's not been some grand plan. It's not something that I've calculated from the beginning or along the way. Everything I've done has just been something that I've kind of gone along with and thought *Oh, that would be a good idea*, at the time.

People told me it probably wasn't the best idea to go to Moscow and it probably wasn't the best idea to run that particular marathon, but for me it was. I followed my heart and went off and did it, and that's where everything kind of took off from.

A marathon distance is 26.2 miles. They can come on all sorts of terrain. I didn't actually realise that at the time, I thought all marathons were run on the road, and I actually continued with that belief well into my running career, because I must emphasise that my running begins

49

and ends when I'm actually physically doing it. I don't live running. I live animals and the sanctuary. So I'm not absorbed in running outside of the time that I'm actually doing it. I am your runner that two minutes before I'm due to go out is searching for a sock. The only time I'm really focusing on running is just before I go out and when I'm doing it. When I get back that's job done, and I move on to something else. Running isn't my world by any stretch of the imagination. It's just something I do in the course of the day.

I always thought the idea of a marathon was to get from A to B, from the start to the finish as quickly as possible. That's what my marathon running career started as. I wanted to be able to get round a marathon as fast as I could. I basically just started to train and think, *Well, what do you do to train? What do you need to do to run a marathon well?* Obviously you've got to be able to keep going for 26.2 miles. That doesn't actually seem, when I think about it, that far. It's not that great a distance. The tricky bit comes when you start to up the pace and maintain the pace, and judge the pace, and find that fine balance between being able to run the distance, but get the maximum out of yourself, but not go into debt. People write for my advice, and I always tell them you can lose far more in a marathon than you can ever gain.

For instance, by judging a pace that you can steadily keep for 26.2 miles you're going to do a lot better than if you run 25 miles really quickly and then blow up. I've got a friend, a very good male runner who always wanted to break 2:30 in a marathon. He tells the story of when he was on for a 2:28 finish in the London Marathon, and he absolutely hit the wall, 800 meters from the finish on Birdcage Walk. He just blew up, and it took him nearly ten minutes to get the last 800 meters.

If you get it wrong you will get it wrong big style, and if you're in that much of a debt, where you've put your body to its absolute limit, there is no coming back from it. Nobody's interested in how fast you got to 22 miles and then blew up. No, people are interested in that finish time. So a clever judging of pace is essential. It's a delicate balance between going as fast as you can but being able to maintain it for as long as you can.

That's basically what I always thought marathon running was about, just literally getting from A to B as quickly as possible with a Vegan Runner top on. Promoting that word in a positive light. The logic was, if you are standing on the elite start of a race with 50,000 runners and there are probably 20 women, and one of them is wearing a Vegan Runner top, that's got to be good for veganism; that's all it's ever been about for me.

When I started to get really good results in races, half marathons, and pretty good marathon times, I was running for the Vegetarian Cycling and Athletics Club, which I was really happy to do, but a guy in that club, Peter Simpson, approached me and said, 'Look, you're doing really well. You're getting elite starts. You're getting invited to races. You're getting expenses paid on these big starts. The only thing people see when you're running at that level is the club that you're running for, and you're running for VCAC, but why don't we start a vegan running club?'

We talked about it, and we thought it was a great idea, because on championship or elite starts people are extremely vigilant about whether you're getting publicity or advertising products, and obviously something like the London Marathon was heavily entwined with Flora and now Virgin, so they wanted ultimate control of the runners that are going to get the publicity, the runners that are going to get on camera.

Before the race starts they'll go down the line of women with a camera, they'll introduce everybody to the crowd. You can't have something written on your vest that they don't want there because they figure that people are going to see it. So before these races you go into these elite areas, and they actually put a piece of Perspex over the lettering on your clothing,

51

even on your socks, to make sure you're not getting any sort of sneaky publicity. The only way around it is if you're running for an affiliated UK athletics club, you've got to have your club name on your shirt. If your club name is something to do with veganism then it's got to be on your shirt and the lettering's got to be correct, but if you've affiliated that word and that club then you can actually legitimately run with it. So that's when we took it upon ourselves to affiliate Vegan Runners as a proper running club.

For the London Marathon particularly, the elite women start 45 minutes before the rest of the race. So you've basically got the whole of the streets of London cordoned off, and you've got literally 20, 22, 25 women running ahead of the field before all the men, and before the main group of runners. You get this lone shot of me running up towards the finish with my vest on. It's just you running alone, 26.2 miles through the streets of London, basically wearing a billboard promoting veganism. That's why I do what I do.

There have been some high moments. I remember once in the London Marathon I was coming up to the finish, and I was in 20th place, which was a big result for me, and the crowds had all gathered because not far behind the elite men would be coming, it's right at the business end of the race, and I remember over the tannoy in Hyde Park the guy just shouting, 'And oh here we have a woman, come on Vegan Runner, come on Vegan Runner'. Everybody was screaming, 'Come on Vegan Runner', because that's all they can see. They can't see your name, they see Vegan Runner, or your number.

That was a pretty awesome moment, just to get that word that we're so passionate about out in a positive way, that people can relate to. People can't get a handle on your name, they don't know who you are, but they can get that word, and it's had such an impact.

52

CHAPTER 10

Full-On Marathons and Training

MY FIRST FULL MARATHON was the Moscow Marathon. I think I chose the Moscow Marathon because I wanted to go somewhere very quiet to see what it was like.

When we arrived there they gave us an interpreter to take us around. It was before the days of the oligarchs in Russia; it was a very austere time to be visiting Russia. You were actually literally kept in one hotel. This dreaded hotel, called the Rossiya Hotel, which was a bit like an enormous prison. You weren't even allowed to go back to your room in the daytime. They had what they called key dragons at the end of every corridor. That's what they called these ladies in charge of the keys. When you went out you had to hand your key to one of the dragons. If you wanted to go back to your room in the day it was viewed with great suspicion, and you were chaperoned around Moscow. You were never allowed to be alone.

When I first went into my hotel bedroom I was quite shocked, I remember the first thing I thought was, *Why is there an enormous freezer in my bedroom? That's very strange.* Then I turned the tap on and all this brown stuff came out so I thought, *No, that's a no-go.* When I saw the plug hanging off the wall my immediate thought was, *Okay, there's a little bit of a death trap going on here. How many sheets have I got on my bed in case I need to knot them together to get out of here if there's a fire?*

I remember in the race I was so shocked at the amount of stray dogs and cats around, literally overrunning the course right into Red Square that I spent most of my time tripping over myself trying to help them. It was just awful. But in the end I came in 10th in that marathon.

So that was my introduction to international races. But everyone told me to do London. Because you can do well in these lower-profile races but it's not going to get you anywhere, publicity-wise. So that's where I figured, okay, I'll go and do the London Marathon. I'll see if I can do all right in that race and that will get the publicity we want, and we'll affiliate the club, and it will all be great from there.

Unfortunately, it didn't really happen like that. I did do well in the race, but again after that race was about that time I went to try and look for a coach and think, *Okay, I've run sub three hours, that's all right, but I now need to get quicker. Obviously that's not good enough, so I need to improve.*

I got a kind of taste for—not winning, because I'm never going to win the London Marathon, I'm not deluded—but doing better. I thought *Okay, I've run like 2:50-odd on my own, what can I do with a coach? What can a coach teach me that I'm not doing?*

I approached quite a lot of people and it was actually quite hurtful because that's when they said, 'You're doing well. You're running good times. You've got the place in London. There's a good base there, but not on the vegan diet. That's not going to happen. We're not going to invest our time in you when you're just going to walk away and do something detrimental to the effort we're putting in'.

There's a real big stereotype here, even in sport. It's terrible in sport. They do think that you need animal-based proteins. There is still a great belief in that.

So I decided to go it alone, with the help of my treadmill. I formulated my own training program, and it wouldn't work for everyone, but it works to me. I'm very basic in what I do. It's what I call the no-frills budget training plan. The only thing that isn't economical in it is effort and mileage, and I think a lot of people do tend to want to hear when they're running 'What's the trick? What's the key?' There isn't a trick. It is going to hurt.

It might be for some people that they can run their best marathon on three light training sessions a week, but it's not going to work for me, and it's not going to work for the majority. It doesn't work for the really elite runners that I've spoken to. It is hard graft at the top. When you see that performance that they're giving it appears to come effortlessly, but behind the scenes at the training camps on a daily basis it isn't easy, it's a lot of hard mileage coupled with speed work on a regular basis.

One of the keys to training for a race—an endurance race or any race—is that it's not how much training you can do on one given day, it's not about oh I can do this mileage, or this distance, or this speed. It's about how quick you can recover and do it again.

I've always trained for a quick road marathon. I didn't do massive mileage, I was doing between about 80 and a 100 miles a week, but that would be every week, for 10 weeks. And you could set your watch by what I was going to be doing any given time, any given day during that period, that 10-week intense cycle getting to a marathon.

I would be doing a speed session on Tuesday morning, and a moderate, easy mileage of eight, ten miles that evening. The next day I would do what I call a long mid-week run, which was about 16 or 17 miles. Thursday, another speed session, another light run in the evening. Friday, hill session, decent mileage, 13, 15 miles. Again on Saturday, a speed session, evening run, slightly less, probably 10K.

On Sunday I would do a longer, steady run of anything from 22 to possibly an over-distanced run of 28 miles. And that would be week in, week out, absolutely no excuses. That's the one thing I am, a no-excuses runner. I don't make excuses for my knee—obviously it does slow me down, and it is extraordinarily difficult to run with—but I'm not going to make excuses for it.

You are what your time is, and I'm not into hiding behind anything else. But I have always realised that it's the consistency of your training that will get you through that race at the time you want. It's no good sporadically saying, 'Oh I did 120 miles that week'. Yeah, but if you haven't been able to train for three weeks after it, that's no good.

It's just judging yourself, knowing what you can get away with—and that's what I think people don't understand about the plant-based diet. It's about having a body, and a constitution, and a physiology, and a mental state that will allow you to do that on a regular basis. That's my 'trick' if you want to run in a quick time in a marathon.

When I did my first marathon in Moscow I was a complete idiot. I literally just thought *I've run 13 miles, 15 miles, I can do that, so I can go and run a marathon.* I didn't realise that you need to train regularly at 20 miles, and the couple of miles you do run after that will be the benefit from the training. A marathon doesn't start until you get to 20 miles, if you're racing seriously. If you really want to maintain it and get through to 26.2 miles with a decent time without blowing up, that's when your training starts. So you will go out on a Sunday and you'll run the first 20 miles knowing that it's the last two or four or six that are going to be the real benefit on the day.

Running wasn't really impacting my leg massively, painfully, up to a half marathon. It's when you get that solid jarring of one pace on one terrain over a couple of hours that you go into debt. When your muscles become weaker—and that's not just your leg muscles, that's your arms, your heart, everything—when you do any exercise over two hours everyone is going to go into some sort of physical debt. It's a question of how well your body can cope with being in that debt—that's the key. And that's what marathon running is really all about, what endurance sport is really all about: how much you can take, how much your body can be trained and prepared to take.

That's why even in my longer training runs I never run an awful lot slower than I intended to race on the day. My Sunday morning runs are always done at a certain time, if I can possibly work it around the sanctuary. You're tricking your mind to think as well, when you set off flat out, or as flat out as you dare, and you think *I've got to keep this going for two hours and 40-odd minutes*, or whatever you're intending to run. That is a big ask. But what your body needs to be able to settle is for your mind to be ready for it. *Hang on a minute, this is what I do on a Sunday. I go out and I feel pain.* That's why I've always made it hurt in training, because I know then it's just going to be normal and natural in racing when it hurts. That's been my logic behind it. Perhaps a coach would have said, 'Oh no, no, no, no, you don't need to go out and beat yourself every week and every session', but that's what I've always thought would benefit me.

When I did my first marathon I was all over the place when I finished. I don't know what I was thinking. It was *hard*. I wasn't prepared for the kind of problems you get when you're unprepared for a marathon after about 20 miles. I just wasn't prepared for what I was going to have to deal with after the race. And I realised, very quickly, that I hadn't done the miles for it. You can get by in a half marathon. It's not that long. It's going to be an hour and 15, 20 minutes, whatever, you can get by. But there's nowhere to hide in a marathon. If you're not ready for it, you're going down and you're going down big time.

I got to the finish line, and I did well enough, but I paid a very high price. It was really hard work, and after that race my body was telling me I'd pushed past my limits. That's when I decided that I had to up my mileage in training and prepare myself better. What I did gain confidence from was the other people in the race—I recovered very quickly, I do recover from things *amazingly* quickly—and some of the poor people I'd gone out there with had to practically be stretchered back onto the plane, they were in such a bad place.

So I realised then that it's not a lost cause, it's something that I needed to build up to and put more mileage in, and work a bit harder at. It was just a learning curve. Every one of my races has been a learning experience.

I think if you are not constantly accepting that you don't know everything, and you are nervous, and you've got the adrenaline running through your veins, then that's probably the time to pack up, because if you're taking things for granted, you can put yourself into dark zones even in marathons.

I have run next to people in road marathons that have died. I remember I went to the Nottingham Marathon and I'd gone there with a fire service group to raise funds for the fire service, and tragically it happened to a guy next to me; a young guy who looked relatively fit. I mean he was in the fire brigade, so he had at least the level of fitness that you've got to attain to be in the fire service. There's a lot of this masculinity and 'I can do it. I can do it' kind of thing.

I was kind of keeping myself to myself, running with these colleagues, and this guy kept complaining that he'd got chest pain. And I said, 'You really should consider slowing down or pulling up for a break', but he insisted it was indigestion, and of course all these guys that I was out there with had had a full English breakfast before they ran, so they were saying it could be indigestion. I was wary because it seemed to me he was rubbing his chest over his heart an awful lot. And during that marathon he had a heart attack and died. He was twenty-seven.

You do get fatalities, even in road marathons, because people are pushing themselves beyond the limit, unprepared. It's a big ask to challenge your body to do that. It doesn't sound that long, two, three, four hours, but it is a long time, and you've got to be well prepared for it. The key is having a body that will allow you to be well prepared for it, because some people just haven't got that recovery rate. I do believe that my diet has had a big factor in this.

CHAPTER 11

Training to Win

I TAKE THE RESPONSIBILITY of my running quite seriously, but I don't take running itself seriously in the way a lot of other athletes tend to. My body is not my temple, and I'm shocked at the amount of people who have massages and physio and stuff like that. And the more I go out there and see runners who do take their running very seriously the more I feel like a real fraud. I have an almost cavalier approach to my running in that way. It's really jumbled—I'm ultra-serious about my bit of it, but I'm not that serious about what it gets me. When I do something, I want to do it really well, because if I'm going to train for an hour that hour is going to be away from the animals. In that hour I'm training I could be working at the sanctuary, with the animals or doing admin. So if I'm going to dedicate an hour or two to something, I've got to be doing it full on or it's not worth me doing it.

I think I probably take the parts of running seriously that other people don't take that seriously and I don't take seriously the parts of running that they do take seriously. For instance, I'm not a big gadget runner; I don't have a pulse monitor, I don't have a Garmin, I don't have any of those things. I kind of figure that whatever computer you have on your wrist, it's not going to be as good as that one that's in your head. You are going to know your own body and your own mind much better than something that's bleeping away and telling you to go a bit faster or go a bit slower, your heart rate's up. Because that can't possibly know if say I've had a stressful morning or I've got a slight chill coming on or I don't feel right. So my running is all coming from inside of me, it's very much personal to me. Because I don't have anyone else's input.

I think I started to take it seriously when I decided I wanted to do a little bit better and perhaps train for a sub three hour marathon; then a sub two fifty marathon; then a sub two forty marathon. And for every minute you cut at that level the margin for error is less and less and less and less. So if you were to say 'I can run four fifteen in a marathon and I want to get it sub four', that's a big ask. It's a big challenge. But it's not as big a challenge as to say 'I can run sub three in a marathon, now I want to run sub two fifty'. The extra effort that goes into that ten minutes is completely disproportionate to the ten minutes. It gets much more intense to gain a few seconds here and there.

Probably about twelve years or so ago I started to really think to myself, right, this is obviously not just about going out there and doing lots and lots of mileage. That is not going to make me quicker. It is going to make me stronger for sure and it might increase my pace a little bit, but it's not actually going to get the giant steps forward that I want. So I suppose when I started hitting the speed work very hard, that's when I started to take it more seriously. To jump up to the next level, sub three, sub two fifty level.

But I do have a problem with the speed work—and the minute I say how I do my speed work all the really hardcore running snobs turn away and look down on me. I've got this knee problem that to an outsider may not appear to be a problem but it is, always, a massive problem to me that I can't really articulate. One of the things that I cannot do is track work. Any track work. I cannot run on a track. It's because I can't run bends. I cannot literally put that input through my knee, that kind of hard pressure that you need to get around the bends on a track. I have tried running on a track and I came back after one session knowing it's not going to work for me, it never was going to work for me. Even if I try running the track in reverse, my knee can't take it. It *will* mess it up.

So I do it all on a treadmill. Which, when you think about it, is still speed, but it's speed in a straight line. That's how I have to do my speed work, which is unconventional and I know people think treadmill running isn't actually that great, and perhaps it isn't. I wouldn't dream of doing all my marathon training on a treadmill because I think I'd crumble with the boredom of it, but my speed work I have to do on there because there's simply no other way.

Especially running alone. I know I could go out on a road and I could run in a straight line perhaps, but it's hard to push yourself to the level that a treadmill does, because in essence, if you crank it up to that pace there's nowhere to hide—you're going to come off the back if you can't hang the pace. It works for me, but a lot of people find it kind of suspect. So I am still extremely amateur in my training and I do things that even basic club runners wouldn't consider doing.

I don't think I've ever had—touch wood—any running injuries. I've had situations where I find it difficult to run because my knee has decided that, hang on a minute, I don't want to do this. But I do run through niggles. I do tend to go out if I've got a niggle, and because I haven't got any real medical or physio or any kind of professional backup, I tend to use this diagnosis method where if I go out and it continues to hurt I'll stop, and if I go out and it stops hurting I'm okay. Because at the end of the day there isn't any pressure on me, I'm not doing it for any other reason than to raise awareness and positivity for veganism so hey, if I come a cropper then okay, I'll just come back in and I'll look after the animals. It's not a big deal. So in that way I don't take running that seriously even now. I don't get all the running magazines or read the blogs or follow people on social media. I don't actually know what half of it is and I don't keep up with it. I haven't got the money for it, I haven't got the time for it.

I don't even warm up. I don't do any stretching exercises—I haven't got time. Once, we were on the elite start of the London Marathon. It's a huge deal, you've got the camera crews, you, the elite women, are going to be the first runners off, and for those 45 minutes the camera crews have got no other runners, they've got nothing else to focus on, so you've got to be the focus of attention for that first bit of the race. And I remember the camera crew that were filming saying to me, 'Aren't you going to warm up? Aren't you going to do something before you set off?' And I'm watching these women going through these elaborate stretching routines and I thought, *If I do something now I'm likely to have a terrible accident and pull a muscle, because this is not what I normally do.*

Here at home I'm normally quite stretched up, because my day never stops and when I stop running I just go off and do something else physical. So I'm always quite flexible. Before I do my running I've climbed fences and I've done all sorts of lifting and weights and I've unloaded loads of hay. But I don't do anything beyond the sanctuary work before running.

But you know, I went off and I did really well in the London Marathon. So it's not a bad thing for me. Some people say it's really inspiring to know that I do that because that's what they do. In the same way it was really inspiring for me to talk with Haile Gebrselassie and he'd tell me the same thing. 'I don't enjoy my training, I don't enjoy the two sessions I do a day'—he's fitting in morning and evening sessions in a full day of business. So you're looking up to people like that who are the greats, the fantastically talented legends of running and you're thinking, *Crikey, if there's one tiny little bit of their life that actually has bearing on mine that's amazing.*

Sometimes I do these public talks and it's all a jumble. I'm not quite sure what I'm supposed to be talking about. I can only tell people who I am and what I have done and what works for me. And I can't give much advice. For the people that ask, I can only tell them what *I* do before a race, which is very little, actually. And the only thing I can say is you can't suddenly race differently than you train, that's the whole point of the training. Keep it as natural to racing as you can. So for instance, don't suddenly in a race think, *Right, I need to take gels, I need to do this, I need to do that.* Because obviously if your stomach's not used to them you should stick to what it knows. Stick to as basic a routine as you have in training, just embellish it slightly with a bit of tapering for a race. That's the only advice I can give.

My day starts very early, and it doesn't ever really stop. I very rarely switch my mind off what I'm doing at the moment. I'll have ideas in the middle of the night that I have to put down on paper or type out. My day has always started very early because I used to work in London in merchant banking. I used to cycle into work, and have to be in by half past seven. I lived 30 miles outside of London so I'd have to leave really early to cycle in and get there on time. So the only time that I knew that I could either get to the gym or train or be on my bike or whatever was before work, so I'd get up at half past three. And that has stuck with me.

I like to get up early. I'm wide-awake then and if I was to fall back to sleep then I would be falling back to sleep until too late. So I like to get up early and I start with the sanctuary jobs. It differs; at one time we had a lot of dogs in the house, and they needed a lot of intensive care. It used to take me about two hours in the morning to hand out medications, clean them up, make sure they were okay. Now I do admin in the morning; I don't want to wake everybody up in the house because my elderly parents live here. And I tend to fit the day around what has to be done, so if I've got a big feed delivery I have to adjust my plan.

But basically my day is all about getting the animals seen to. I have to know in my head that the animals and everything that surrounds the animals—and that's vets visits, that's farrier visits, dentist visits, taking them off-site to vets, everything that encompasses looking after 400 animals—is set. Visiting the five other yards, seeing the deliveries at the other yards, interacting with the people who own the other yards. All of that takes a lot of time. So the training has to be fitted in around that as and when I can.

If I haven't trained during the day, I might go out during the night with a head torch. That's completely okay to me. It's not something I used to particularly think of doing and it's not probably ideal for a high tempo run because no head torch can match running in daylight, so you've got to watch yourself and I'm extremely wary of a trip or anything going wrong with my right leg. I really don't want to come a cropper unnecessarily.

But the main motivation for me to get out and run is usually, in some way shape or form, lack of time. That is, I'll be looking at my watch and thinking *If I don't get out now, it's not going to happen.* Once I get out there

I'll want to actually do the training I'm supposed to be doing. So if I want to do an 18 mile run I know that's going to take me just under a couple of hours, and if I'm seeing the clock and the time disappear, that's what makes me grab my gear and go. And I'll be tired but I know that I'll beat myself up if I don't go, and since I'm damned if I do and damned if I don't, I just fit it in.

What I have to do each day is always there in my head, and I sometimes wake up and feel so bad that I do kid myself and tell myself, 'No, you feel so awful today, skip running. Don't run today, you don't need to train today'. Then as the day goes on I think, *No, you do need to train today, you really should, it's not that bad.* And I go out. Because I know being unprepared in a race is probably the worst thing you can do. It's really hard to put into words, but you can push yourself to the limit and get 100 percent out of yourself, but there is a line and if you cross it, you're taking too much out of yourself and it takes you too long to recover. I've run road marathons that took six weeks to a couple of months to recover from, before I've felt able to run again. And that's only 26.2 miles, that's a flat road race. You can feel better when you finish, and then a couple of weeks later it will suddenly hit you. You can push yourself over and beyond, where you're really putting yourself in a danger zone.

So I like to be as prepared as I can for running, and that, for me, is running a lot of miles, fitting that in, and by doing that I know when I come to my taper I've done all I can, there's nothing more I could have done. I don't want to be looking back and think, if I'd not missed that long run on that day.... I like to know that that's 'job done' regarding the actual training.

Then the admin work, that's quite heavy actually because with the sanctuary we like to be very personal. Now I'm going to say that my running has been to promote veganism, it hasn't been to promote Fiona and I'm not sitting here thinking I haven't got the rewards I deserve. For example, years ago a vegan group in Sweden contacted us and they said 'We've seen that picture of you in the London Marathon coming down the Mall with the Vegan Runners top on and we love it, and we're doing a billboard campaign in Stockholm to promote veganism. Can we use that image for the poster?' Then they said, 'But the only thing is we can't use your name, it's got to be the image without the name', and I said 'Why would that bother me? That's all I've ever wanted, the image, the vegan word getting out there in a positive way'. And that's truly it.

So with the running side of the admin work, people write to me and they want my advice and to do that takes me quite a long time, because if people write and ask for my help, as much as is physically and humanly possible I want to be able to help them. That's what my running is about, it's not about telling people how great I am, because I'm not. It's about helping them to be as great as they can be. That's what's important to me. Admin can take a long time because two or three hours can go by when you're just busy reading people's emails, reading them properly and answering their specific questions, rather than just sending them a 'Hi, thanks for your support' reply mail. I don't want to do that. I really do like to speak to them.

So that takes a long time, but that has to come secondary to the animals. Bearing in mind I've got 61 horses, and we're lucky in that we've got land where a lot of them free roam, we've got big shelters, and I would say I probably spend eight, nine hours outside a day visiting the other yards, making sure that the horses are mucked out, cleaned, cared for, medicated.

If the blacksmith or the farrier's here, it can be longer, because I've literally got to stand by the horses and hold them while the blacksmith or farrier does their work. Or for instance last year, I went down to one of the other yards, everything was fine when I left them the night before, but when I arrived early in the morning one of the horses, Rose, was staggering around with blood coming from her nostrils and her mouth, and I couldn't work out what had happened.

We still don't fully know what happened, the vet couldn't tell us, but I was down there from about seven in the morning to half past seven at night, when sadly Rose had to be put to sleep. And that means I'm going to work all night to catch up with everything else. So it's extremely hard to quantify, but the main part of my day is spent outside administering to the animals. Which actually does not help the running at all, because very often I go out running and I am very, very tired. I'm not actually recovered when I'm running, I never feel fresh when I go out running. I can run ten miles where it's absolutely diabolical, it can take me that long to hit my stride. I tend to get stronger towards the end of a run—probably because I can sniff the finish line, so to speak, and I know it's going to stop.

But I am very often running on tired limbs and legs. And when I've trained for marathons I've trained so intensely and religiously and with such discipline that I've literally gone down the drive and I've been crying, sobbing, thinking *I just don't know if I can get through this*. I know physically I should be able to but mentally, the going is so tough. It's so hard and it's so bleak and you always want to hit your targets because a poor run is almost worse than no run at all; not being able to do what you want to do or not be able to think you're progressing in the right direction. And I haven't got anyone to tell me otherwise, I haven't got a coach helping me psychologically, I've only myself to wrestle with.

So the admin has to come last, but it's always there, and I'm always thinking about it. Very often I use the running to think, to pass the time, because I don't train with music or anything like that, so I'll be thinking about how I'm going to address people and how I'm going to answer their questions. So it's kind of doubly productive.

CHAPTER 12

Base Preparations

I'VE DONE A REALLY WIDE range of things with my marathon running, and when people ask me what the hardest marathon I've run is, they probably do not expect my answer. Obviously it is extremely hard to go and run, crawl, whatever you're going to do, through Marathon des Sables for seven days, that is a tough experience full stop. But honestly, I have to say running a quick marathon is probably harder for me, because there is absolutely no let-up for the time you're there. You start training four to five months before that race and you are focusing on one Sunday morning at 9 o'clock, a specific date, a specific time when you have got to be right to deliver the goods. And that is hard. There is no breaking and seeing if you feel better the next day. There is absolutely not an inch of room for maneuvering if you want to get the best out of yourself.

And it's hard to train for it. It's brutal to train for it. It might be easier if you're training with a group and you've got a lift, you're meeting people, you've got specific goals, you've got specific occasions, like track sessions. The self-motivating to do that on your own is tremendous. That's what a lot of people have been impressed that I've been able to do, self-motivate like that.

Then if you can get through the training period, you come to the taper period, which is a nightmare for you and it's a nightmare for those around you. And there's not a lot I can do professionally, I can't just withdraw from the sanctuary and go away and live somewhere like a hermit as a lot of runners do before they actually want to run a fast road run. So I have to stay here at the sanctuary. Down the yard we have a caravan, and that caravan is there for when I've been running fast marathons. I used to go and live in the caravan when Martin came home from work so that I didn't risk him bringing anything home like a flu or cold—you can't have *any*thing in a marathon. You certainly can't have anything systemic.

You literally want to wrap yourself in cotton wool, but I can't because I've got the animals to look after. So I just have to withdraw as much I can, and that means living like a hermit down there in the caravan and making sure I don't come into contact with anyone. And every morning you'll wake up and convince yourself you've got a sore throat. This isn't just me, this is what other runners will tell you. Because you've invested so much into this short period of time, this sub three hour run or whatever you're aiming to do on that Sunday morning.

There's not any sense of joy, particularly, when I finish these races, it's just relief that I've managed to get there and do it.

Here's a really graphic example. I trained really, really hard and heavily for Marathon des Sables in 2012, and the week before I went out there I was alone at the sanctuary, I was doing the jobs. And an elderly horse, a 42-year-old thoroughbred horse that we had here, Charity, she went down. For anybody who knows horses they know that a horse cannot be down for very long. Charity had an injury, that's why she came to the sanctuary in the first place. So it was doubly important that she get to her feet quickly. And I couldn't find anyone available to come help, so I had to help her up, and she got up, for which I was thankful—but as she did she stepped backwards and stepped on my foot and broke two toes. The week before I went to the toughest foot race in the planet. So the injuries can happen.

There are some funny stories. One of the times I was training for the London Marathon, this one guy said to me, 'Fiona, you know I love athletics,' and I'm thinking, *But how do I know? You're not giving me any vibe that you love athletics, Jeff.* He said, 'I can get you these running shoes at trade price'. And I asked him 'What're you going to do? Get me a pair of clogs for free and expect me to run round in them? I've got specific things that I do need and I can't run in that particular brand of running shoes'. And he actually said to me, 'Well if they're causing you trouble, can't you stop at 20 miles and change them and put a new pair on?'

And I'm thinking, *Are you seriously telling me that you know about running and you're suggesting that at* 20 miles *in a road marathon* I stop and I change my shoes? *Please.* Did you not see what Paula Radcliffe was forced to do, and sadly remembered for doing, in the London Marathon one year because she simply did not want to break her rhythm? And you're suggesting I stop and change my shoes at the side of the road? Is that what people's idea of running a marathon is? I don't know.

The one thing I do need is a cushioning for my knee, so I do tend to change my shoes regularly. After about 300 miles, a pair of trainers, even though they may look okay, they're pretty much dead. And they do kind of fall apart in these stage races. You can't do too much in them. I mean, one stage race and that's a pair of shoes gone. You wouldn't want to be wearing them again. You're lucky if you can find a pair of shoes that you're comfortable in, because when you're trying to run quickly, you really don't want problems with your feet. That's the one part of your body you do not want to be having an issue with, whether you're running a fast marathon, or a slower marathon, or a marathon off-road, for me, it's the most important thing.

Once when I went to Berlin, I was with this guy in the hotel and he said, 'No, I've got everything for the race start. I've got my lucky trainers'. And I looked at him and I thought, *You're going to run in those?* They looked absolutely clapped out, and because I did well in that race and he didn't, I told him if he wanted to run a quicker marathon I thought he really had to concentrate a little bit more on his feet, instead of on this extravagant nutrition that he had, which hadn't actually done him any good. A lot of people spend a lot of money on kit because it looks pretty, and it looks nice, and it looks cute. But your feet are the most important thing and, even though a pair of shoes might look okay and they might be okay for regular goings about, they're probably not okay for that absolute pounding the running puts them through. So I try to always pay attention to what I'm putting on my feet, as best as I can.

With marathons it's not so much the number of the people in the race, it's the distance of the race, and they're all 26.2 miles so they're all taken quite seriously. Moscow was a big race because obviously it's a major city marathon in a country that is well into sport. The real major marathons, there were five and now six—Chicago, New York, Boston, Berlin, London, and now in Japan they've got a major marathon in Tokyo. But I would consider my first big marathon London, in 2004. That was the one that I specifically wanted to get sub three hours in, do well in. And it was because of running London that we set up the Vegan Running club. When we discovered how these elite starts worked and that there was real potential for publicity for veganism, we wanted a specific running club. That's when we decided that this was a real thing that we could do to promote it in a positive way and get the word out there.

All the marathons I've run have been pretty major events in my life because they're all such a long way and it's so hard. That saying about how a marathon starts at 20 miles is probably the truest thing I've ever heard. You really don't want to be struggling up to 20 miles, because you're *really* going to struggle after and you don't want to perpetuate that struggle any longer than you have to.

That being said, London in 2004 was my first *major* major one. And it was a very positive experience. I think it was my first time thinking, yes, I could probably do a good job with running. It was positive for many reasons: I ran way under championship qualifying time, I got a sub three, I got a good place in the race, and I also got on TV beforehand. BBC interviewed me before the race, so it was like ting, ting, ting, ticked all the boxes. And from that race we formed the Vegan Runners. The race showed hey, this is really something we can do, so we got a plan together. So that was probably the most positive results I could have had.

It was tough though. I mean all my runs have been tough because I put my heart and soul into them. I think, for me, especially with running road marathons when I was trying to get competitive times and get big results, if anybody had said to me it was easy, then I'd say well then you didn't do well. You didn't get the max out of yourself, because no way should it be easy out there. You know you're going out there to put yourself through it, you just hope you can put yourself through it for the right amount of time to get the result and end up at 26.2 miles, spent but not overspent. Not in debt too much.

So London Marathon in 2004, yes, it went well. But they're hard. I've never been married but people say it's like a wedding. You plan for it and you're so focused on it all going well that you wish you could go back and enjoy it. I haven't really enjoyed all these races because you're aware, as you are in training, that at any point you can hit this wall, it can go wrong, the wheels can come off, and if the wheels come off in a marathon there is simply no way of getting them back on. That is just the end of it. So you're always running on nerves and adrenalin and desire.

I remember in 2009 I was doing the London Marathon to raise some funds for Captive Animals' Protection Society—I'm a patron, and I said I would run to raise funds for them. I wasn't feeling that great on the race day, let's put it like that. I'd had a lot on at the sanctuary and we'd had a lot of bad weather. But I wanted to do it because I was raising the funds for the society, and I remember coming down Cannon Street about four or five miles to go to the finish. And you are starting to think, even though five miles doesn't *sound* very long, it's only 8K, it can seem like forever when you know you've got a certain pace to hit. You need to be able to keep hitting that pace or you're just going to go backwards. And like I said you can lose far more time in a marathon that you can ever hope to gain.

What I mean by that is if you can run six minute miles, to run five minutes fifty-five second miles is going to take an awful lot of effort but it's only going to give you a couple of minutes in the race. So it's really hard to gain a couple of minutes but it is so easy to lose a lot more than a couple of minutes, trust me. Like the friend of mine who was running for 2.28 in London and he ended up with 2.38. He lost 10 minutes in 800 meters. It can go horribly wrong. People say, 'Oh, you must have been able to' and you literally can't. Imagine this scenario. Somebody has got a gun at your head and they're saying, 'Unless you run faster I am going to shoot you' and it's like you've got to say, 'Well shoot me then because I just can't'. There's nothing else there to be had.

All that being said though, there really is a huge mental aspect to it. I remember I was running down Cannon Street in London, and I don't know why I looked up at this particular point, because I was so focused on the running, on the road, but I did. And I saw that somebody had put a banner across the road, and it said something like 'Fiona, doing it for the animals. Vegan proud'. And I just saw the words 'Fiona' and 'vegan proud' and I felt so humbled it must have lifted me that extra gear that I couldn't find in myself.

CHAPTER 13

Impact

AFTER A WHILE I DECIDED to switch gears with the running. Obviously I knew I wasn't going to ever win the London Marathon or win Berlin. So I decided, okay, I'll look at the next tier down, look at races that I probably can win, make a bit more local impact, a bit more impact in this country.

We have the big county athletics championship race, the Halstead Marathon, and it's fairly local to me, so I decided that I was going to enter this race and do well in it and see if winning a race would make any more impact than a top 20, or top 10 could in these major city races. So I trundled along to this race and it was a fairly big marathon and I always travel with my mum, purely because you need someone there with you just to pick you up at the finish or to articulate the fact that you're in trouble to emergency services or whatever. She likes to be there to support me and also I think it's kind of educational for people to see, for parents to see a parent there that *has* been accepting of a vegan child who's now grown into a vegan adult, who's become very successful as a vegan adult in an extreme athletic performance field. So my mum was there with me and the usual way of things is that I set off and my mum just waits for me to finish. This race is not known for quick times, it's a really difficult, hilly kind of race, a 'tough man' race. It's been running for about 25 years now.

So I set off and when I was out running she was speaking to one of the town councillors, the lady who was actually going to present the prizes. And she asked, 'Who've you got out there running?' People tend to think it's going to be a husband or son, but Mum told her 'My daughter', 'Oh really? Which one's she?' 'Oh she's the one with the Vegan Running top'. 'Oh she's a vegan?' Mum said, 'Yes, she's been vegan since she was a small child'. And the lady said, 'Oh, my daughter wants to go vegetarian but I'm not so sure it's a good idea because she's only 14 and we're concerned about whether it'll be detrimental to her growth, how it's going to affect her in later life. It's quite pivotal, when they're just going from childhood to adulthood'. And Mum said, 'Well it's not affected my daughter, she's out here today'. And the lady was like, 'Oh right, that's fine. What's your daughter come to do?' And Mum couldn't very well say to her, 'Oh she's come to win and she's come to break the course record and she's going to prove that a woman can run under three hours on this course even though it's never been done'. She couldn't really say that, so she said, 'Oh, we'll wait and see'.

So when we were coming in to the finish line, there's a couple of guys finished and then somebody shouted out, 'There's another runner coming through'. And then somebody said, 'Oh, it's a woman' and sure enough it was me coming along, and I did everything I wanted to do. I won, I ran under three hours, and I still hold a course record from that race, 10 years on. And when the councillor presented me with the prize she said to me, 'I had a long chat with your mum. You are just so amazing. If it's any comfort I've got no worries at all now about letting my daughter go vegetarian after seeing what you've just done in this race'.

That to me was like the biggest prize ever. You can forget the cheque, you can forget the trophy, you can forget the medal or whatever. That was the biggest prize ever. And that's what really made me think, more than going and winning a race and it being something to brag over others, 'I won and you came second', that was what it was about. That's probably the key. By doing well in races it would have that kind of result. And that's been my trophy from running, not the times or anything else. That has been the big prize that I've always been trying to attain with my running and that's what keeps me going and keeps me running, being able to do that.

CHAPTER 14

Rovaniemi

THERE IS A STORY BEHIND doing Rovaniemi in 2010. I had intended to do a much bigger marathon in May. I hadn't been very well in April. There was nothing particularly wrong with me apart from the fact that my elderly pony, Max, was coming to the end of his life. And I knew it, I knew it in my heart. We'd had an episode with him in November and the vet had said, 'Perhaps it might be time to look at putting him to sleep', but I knew that wasn't the time for him to go to sleep. He had a colic one Sunday morning, the vet came out, she did everything she could for him and she said, 'Let's monitor him for three to four hours and if he's no better I'll have to come back and put him to sleep'. And after three hours she started to ring, and I said, 'Don't answer the phone because he's not ready, he's not ready'. And sure enough he recovered from that.

But that winter, it'd become his natural time. He was very old. And I was supposed to go off to this bigger race, but I couldn't go. Because

I just felt wrong, I just felt wrong and I realise now that it felt wrong because the bigger race was actually held the week before Max died. I know that I would have never forgiven myself for leaving him and building up to this race and doing everything on that intense level when I needed to spend that time with him and help him. And help myself through his passing.

So I had this energy for running a marathon but I hadn't got anywhere to run a marathon. That's when I decided I would go to this race in Finland. The Rovaniemi Marathon is this big road marathon just below the Arctic Circle that they hold up there. It's actually where they do a lot of the Santa festivities. They have this big running festival and it's quite a big event in Finland, and it culminates in this marathon.

I went up there and I suppose I was only going half-heartedly to get this frustration and energy and grief out of myself. But I ran this really quick time and broke the course record and everybody was super shocked that this person who just turns up and doesn't particularly look like a marathon runner then suddenly goes and hits it hard and finishes with the men. It was all very surreal to be honest with you. Again I suppose I'd gone to win, which I did, that was the job done. But more than that is that I was asked to speak after it, to speak on behalf of veganism. They realised that they'd got a big problem because one of the prizes for the race was a reindeer skin and people had actually clocked the fact that oh God, she's a vegan. They didn't know what to do. Up on one of my shelves is this beautiful hunting knife that they gave me instead. Which was like, What am I going to do with that coming through customs? A great big machete thing.

But to me, more than going and winning and breaking a course record, it's that platform it gives you, to explain to people within this field who take their diets very seriously, why you've run and, to their amazement, why you don't eat animal products. They've been told in magazines and articles and everywhere that you need animal protein to be successful. And you're coming and beating them and you don't eat that. That's why I selected these races. To actually be able to go and do well in them, hopefully, and then be able to sort of reel people in, rather than grab them and force them in and push them in—make them actually want to start asking questions.

In Rovaniemi I'd come and I'd done so well and they were like, 'Could you talk to our running clubs afterwards? Could you do a lot of media afterwards? This is so unusual to us.' They treat their running quite seriously out there. That's more why I strategically chose these races. I did another one, Levi, a really tough one in Finland again, that I won. A similar sort of thing. Just to give me that platform from which to be able to interact with people who are interested. You've got this invested audience—people who are in a race generally want to do well in it, they're always looking for ways of doing better in those races and diet obviously is a big focus. Training and diet, and equipment to a certain extent, are the main points of running.

So if you've got this alternative lifestyle then you've got this invested audience to speak to and hopefully they'll take this away to other races. I found this in the stage races as well, a lot of the guys, especially from Scandinavian countries, are really interested in the plant-based way of living and improving in sport. And I'm seeing that growing now. That's mainly the reason that I've actually done these things.

I set the Rovaniemi course record by about half an hour. If people ask about it though, I do tend to brush it aside, because I'd gone there to do that, to break the course record. I wouldn't have bothered going if I didn't think I could do it, because my heart, my soul, my mind, my money, everything I've got is here at the sanctuary and it's going to take some huge thing to prize me away to go somewhere else. When I've got backup here, like Martin, if I go away to do a road marathon he's able to look after the animals whilst I'm away for a couple of days, and then the big incentive for going is that I can probably do more good by going than I can by staying. And since I can do an awful lot of good by staying, it's got to be something big to make me go.

It's not a big deal when I've done it, to me. It's just job done. Then I've got to kind of let people know that I've done it, but I always intended that my running would be just an example. It was all born out of frustration that there's this persistent idea that you need these products to make you a complete athlete and without them you cannot reach or raise your maximum potential. I just wanted to show otherwise.

I've got an example. When I did the London Marathon in 2005, because you've only got this small group of ladies setting off and running down the road, there's not an awful lot for the commentators to talk about, the camera's just panning across the elite women and that kind of thing. But they do a ring in Q and A, before the elite men start running, 45 minutes down the line. They've got to fill the broadcast time.

So Tracey Morris, a tremendously talented runner, she was doing the Q and A for the BBC with Steve Cram or whoever was commentating on there, and, of course, they were inviting people to ring in with questions and since the focus was on the ladies' elite race, the questions were really geared towards ladies' elite running. Lots of my supporters were calling in but one actually got through and asked, 'Do you think it's possible to run on this start as a vegetarian or a vegan?' And I'm out there in my Vegan Runner top, trudging down the road with these elite runners, and she said no, you would need animal based products to actually be able to be running at this level.

I didn't hear it at the time, I heard it on a recording afterwards, and it's so frustrating that even then, when I was actually right there doing it, the commentator was saying no, it's not possible. And probably in her world, she thought that was the case.

So there still is this massive, massive barrier between the concepts of vegan and high-level athletic performance. There is always this connection that is made between meat and dairy and athleticism. It still is there. It's changing, it is changing, but there's still this deep-seated perception that vegan equals weakness.

But I'd ask how weak is it to be able to walk away from the majority and say, 'Actually, I'm my own person, and this is a really liberating thing'. I mean, you get people saying to you 'You can't have that, can you?' a lot, about foods. But the answer is 'Yes, I can. I can quite easily have that, but I don't want it'. You're taking control of your own life. But getting other people to do that is very difficult. That's why I have felt compelled to keep on with the running, and keep on doing the endurance events whilst I can, doing the kind of things that wouldn't have entered my head even a few years ago. It wouldn't have even entered my head to go to the North Pole or Antarctica. It wouldn't have even occurred to me that there was a marathon there, and if there was a marathon there, that I'd be running it.

CHAPTER 15

The Great North Run

THE GREAT NORTH RUN is the largest half marathon in the world. It's run in Newcastle, Tyneside, and it attracts the best of the best. The best marathon runners and the best shorter distance runners. A full marathon runner can obviously drop down distance and run a half marathon very competitively. For a 10K runner, you can move up to run and bluff your way to a half marathon. So you've got kind of the best of the best in what I would call road athletic endurance events.

I got awarded a place on the elite start; but I was then approached by the Vegan Society, which I'm an honorary patron of, and they said they wanted to make the race a big publicity stunt for promoting veganism in an en masse way, and would I consider running with the Vegan Society team, to promote them? And the answer was 'Yes, for sure.' Because running on the elite start, you're running against people like Tirunesh Dibaba, double Olympic champion at 10,000 meters and you're just going nowhere with that. I didn't particularly care about my time in race, I just want to get maximum publicity for veganism, so I thought running in the Vegan Society team, that's a good idea. So I had to give up my place on the elite ladies start and run off the main start, which starts about 20–25 minutes behind the elite ladies start. But I was granted a place with the elite men, right at the front of the race, which was amazing.

It was really, really funny, actually, because it was raining, absolutely pouring down with rain, and every other runner there, all the elite men, had got their managers and coaches and God knows what with them, and I've had to go to the start on my own, Little Miss Amateur gone mad. I had on my Vegan Runner sweatshirt, because I needed something to keep me warm before the start and I decided I would be able to throw it away later, and then two laundry bags that I had stolen from the hotel to wrap up my legs to keep them warm. So I'm wandering around in the elite enclosure, which is basically the first bit of road that you run down, with all these very professional looking runners around me and I'm in an old sweatshirt with laundry bags around my legs. I'm surprised the security man let me into that enclosure.

It was a really, really horrid day and I had elected quite unusually to run in long sleeves and long running bottoms, which looked like I was on a Sunday morning training run rather than actually turning up for this massive, massive race. They let me in and I'm kind of wandering around and feeling that I should be doing something that looks mildly like I'm interested or like I know what I'm doing, like stretching-wise or warming up-wise, and when I'm thinking, *Oh deary me, I really don't want to do this at all.*

Haile Gebrselassie was running the race, he'd come to break the world record, and Jos Hermens, his coach, arrived early and he recognised me from other races, and we'd been talking, and he told me to come sit in his car since it was raining. So in one minute I'd gone from someone that nobody even wants to know and is like an embarrassment, to sitting in Haile Gebrselassie's car, and everyone's thinking What is going on here? What is this attachment with this weird person? And Jos said to me, 'Look, it's time to go to start now. Would you like to walk up there with Haile and myself?'

So all of a sudden it's Little Miss Amateur walking up to the start of this race with my Vegan Running top on with Haile Gebrselassie and everybody wondering, What is going on? And that is the kind of positive publicity that I was craving. This endorsement, this acceptance, not of me, but my veganism.

So I set off from the start, and won the main start, so I was pleased with that. To say you got top 20 in the Great North Run, off what wasn't the elite start, was a really big thing. I can say now that I won the main start at the Great North Run, which is massive, and I got top 20 in the Great North Run, which I never thought I'd be able to do. It was a good publicity stunt. A good day at the office for the Vegan Society.

But that gesture by Jos and Gebrselassie at the start of the race was brilliant and it was a big lift to my spirits. It was very humbling that Jos had taken the time to ask me if I was okay and kind of reach out to me, because I've always respected Gebrselassie. I've always respected obviously his talent but also his motives for running, and the time he takes for other people.

Another illustration of what kind of man Gebrselassie is was Berlin in 2007. That was another complete disaster. I'd done incredibly well in the Berlin Marathon in 2006, way above my expectations, and they'd invited me back in 2007. But before the race I'd fractured two ribs at the sanctuary, with a ridiculous accident unloading some hay. I was at a point where I couldn't sit up and lay down in bed properly, but I'd gone to the race because I'd got an elite start in the Berlin Marathon with everything there paid for, elite hotel and everything, and to be amongst these runners and to be able to wear that Vegan Runner vest amongst the best runners in the world was very important to me, so I figured I've got to go. These opportunities do not come up that often, so I went. And it wasn't a great experience, trying to run a marathon with two fractured ribs. But beforehand, there again Gebrselassie was so generous with his time, and insisted on the security men giving him a pen so he could write good luck on my top and included me in a documentary that was made about his racing in Holland.

So those little things, they give you a lesson. It does matter, helping other people, encouraging other people, for whatever reason you're encouraging them, whether you're just encouraging them for their running or you're encouraging them that they can do it as a vegan—it matters. Those little things that you can do, do matter, and are important to people.

CHAPTER 16

Finland to Dartmoor

ALWAYS WITH MY RUNNING I've got these little ideas and targets. Goals to reach. My next target was the Levi International Marathon in Finland. I thought, *I'll go there and I'll try to win it; I'll try to place with the men and I'll just go under three hours and that will be okay.* I did all that. I maintained my pace and I did the job that I wanted to do. I won Levi and broke the course record.

I came back home after Levi, and I knew I was going to do Marathon des Sables in 2012, in April, but this was at the beginning of September 2011, and I didn't feel very tired, so I thought I probably had another marathon in me that year. That's when I went off and did Dartmoor, five weeks after Levi.

Dartmoor is a ridiculously tough race. I arrived in Dartmoor and immediately thought, *This isn't a marathon, it's a joke.* Huge hills and tough terrain. It was an appalling race. I thought, *I've made a mistake here.* It's a half marathon, mainly, and the full marathon is two laps of the same course. So the half marathon goes off, the full marathon goes off, and the full marathon does it twice.

When I came up to the finish line for the full marathon, they tried to direct me to go and do another lap. They didn't believe that I'd finished so quickly—thought I must have another lap to do. I was overtaking the actual half marathon runners at the start, going faster than people at the front of the half marathon field, and they were like, 'Are you running the half?' 'No, I'm running the full'.

So I won that one and I broke that course record as well, beat the next runner by about twenty minutes I think, so that was pretty good, because I could then finish that season on a high and get into my training for the Marathon des Sables in 2012.

I'd run Dartmoor as training, with a backpack, because I knew it was a tough marathon—I didn't realise how tough it was, but it was tough in terms of the fact that there was no way you were going to be able to run speed up these ridiculous climbs, I didn't think—so I figured I'd put some weights on and that would be great training for the Marathon des Sables. After I'd won that race in Levi, I thought I'd see if I could go and do well-ish in Dartmoor, and I did. I set off and it just came together for me. I didn't know how long I'd be able to hang onto it, but I knew I was strong. Because I'd became wary about the challenge of MDS. It had suddenly hit me that I'd be running the equivalent of seven marathons in seven days, in extreme heat, in sandy terrain, and I wasn't sure I was prepared for that.

I'd talked with good runners, and they said that Marathon des Sables is completely different. So I was getting a bit edgy about it—have I got the endurance in my legs, have I got the right muscle groups ready, have I got the right mentality, have I got the recovery that you need for that sort of thing? I really didn't know what I was getting into and I hadn't done any over-distance ultra-race up until that point, which is a bit stupid, but, as I say, ignorance is bliss. But as I said, I was becoming a bit edgy about it, so that's why I decided to do Dartmoor with a pack, to try to get a taste of what it would be like to run in a competitive way with a pack on.

CHAPTER 17

Marathon des Sables

THE IDEA FOR MDS WAS planted in 2011, when somebody said to me 'You've won a couple of marathons this year, you've done really well—why not do Marathon des Sables next year?' and I thought, *Oh what's that? I've never heard of that.* Because I am the most unclued-up runner you'll ever meet, I still don't know very much about it at all. But I thought, *Okay I've done fast races, hard fast races, I'll try this. I'll give it a go and see if I can get round it; I'll be the first vegan woman to do this. This is great.*

The Marathon des Sables is billed as the toughest foot race on the planet. It's a week of marathons in the Sahara Desert, and you've got to be self-sufficient, you've got to carry all your own gear. So it's made that much more difficult if you're a vegan, especially at the time, because obviously I'm not having the down sleeping bag, I'm not having the down jackets that are considerably lighter. I'm wearing synthetic products. If you're going to do it ethically as a vegan you've got to have a giant

sleeping bag, because you've got to use a synthetic bag and it's got to be of a certain rating to keep you warm at night (and you get quite cold because you're depleted of energy). No matter how light you go, it's heavy, it's ginormous, it's nearly twice the size of everybody else's and twice the weight.

And at the time, there wasn't the sports replacements foods and bars and drinks they have now. Tiny little bags of porridge that come in at eight hundred and fifty calories that other runners take, I couldn't take because they're not vegan. So I had to make it up with bars and stuff. So all in all I was pretty much doing it on a remarkably amateur basis with this huge pack.

Then, the week before I went out there, I was at the sanctuary alone and one of the elderly horses stood on my foot and broke two of my toes. It couldn't have been worse. I was left wondering, Do I go, or do I stay? And I thought well if I stay, I'm going to be damning myself, because I'll always wonder if I could have got round and done it. So I decided to go.

The problem was, as mentioned, the Marathon des Sables is in the Sahara Desert, and naturally it gets extremely hot out there. They say you need to buy shoes at least a size too big, because if you don't your feet are going to swell and you're going to get blisters. And blisters are the one thing you do not want in that race. I've seen people with the soles of their feet like pieces of raw meat—no flesh on them at all. The race takes place over a week, and I've seen people pull out on the last day because they cannot face 15 more kilometers on feet that are just unbearably painful.

Of course I hadn't got time to change my shoes, they've got to be professionally stitched up with gaiters and Velcro to keep the sand out. There's a lining around the shoe for the Velcro, because when you do these stage races in the desert you don't want even a single grain of sand in your shoes. The sand is absolutely your worst enemy, it really is. You don't want any stitching on the inside—anything in that shoe is going to rub over that week, if it gets contact, and then you're going to get blisters, and then you are not going to be able to walk. So you get these sand gaiters, and they're supposed to stop the sand getting in your shoes. They do, to a certain extent, but if you put them on wrong then it doesn't work, so you've got to be extremely careful with the way you get them on.

So I'm staring at my broken toes and thinking *Okay, I'll go with the shoes I've got. I can just about get them on even with the broken toes.* Unfortunately, my feet did swell when I got out there; they swelled immediately. So now I had shoes that were causing blisters on the first day, and by the fourth day, the longest day, I could hardly bear it. You could see the bone in my little toe, I'd rubbed so much skin off.

The running experience of Marathon des Sables is one week long, but the actual experience of Marathon des Sables is about twelve days, in terms of the fact that you just don't arrive on a start line as you would with a normal race and set off running. There are a lot of checks and pre-race criteria that have to be fulfilled. The running starts on a Sunday and finishes on the following Saturday, but that's not when the race experience starts.

You fly out to Morocco on a plane that the race organisers charter. People from different countries arrive in different ports and we all congregate at this one place. Then you are shipped to an unidentified destination in the desert that changes every year. The reason for that is they do not want to allow cheating, because if you know where the race is going to start and you know the route, you could potentially place aids around the course to help you—food, water, nutrition, medication, things like that, and naturally they don't want that to happen.

You arrive at this unidentified destination, where you see an awful lot of tents in a big circle. Unless you've gone out there with someone or intend to meet someone out there, you're alone. It's often night by the time you arrive, and you wander round the camp in the dark, searching for a tent that appears to have a space in it, which is where you will live for the next week. The tents are old Berber tents, they've got no front and no back. They do not protect you from the elements. They are literally a covering from the sun. You've got the space in the tent in which your bedroll fits and that's your home for the week. And unless you know someone you are then confined with these seven strangers, male or female, for that entire week.

The next day, the Saturday, you go through a rigorous process of what they call race checks, where you are scrutinised, your backpack is scrutinised, the weight of it is scrutinised, and your equipment is scrutinised. It's all quite regimented, and depending on what time of day your bag check is, your civvy bag, your bag with the luxuries of life, could be taken away from you at eight o'clock that morning.

They make sure that you've got 14,000 calories, 2,000 calories a day, to keep you going. It's not enough. It's enough nutrition to get you through, but it's certainly not enough to be comfortable. And then you have everything that you are not going to carry with you on the race taken away from you. That's shipped off back to a hotel somewhere in a local town, and you're then left in the middle of the desert. You wander back into camp and then that's it, you've got nothing apart from what you intend to carry during the race, or what you're prepared to throw away on the morning of the race.

On Sunday morning you get up, you bundle everything up into your pack. You're already wearing your running gear, that's all you've had from the day before. You're rushing to the start.

You're given limited water. You're given your instructions. Big race spiel about what to do, what not to do, how to conduct yourself in the desert. The absolute imperative importance, what you have to do if you do nothing else, is take your salt tablets. If they see a salt line on any of your clothes you are warned and then you're pulled out the race. You're not supposed to be losing fluids and it's the salt that keeps the fluids and keeps you hydrated. You continually drink, but it's just going to go straight through you if you aren't taking the salts to hold it in. A lot people don't actually follow those instructions because there is this ridiculous idea that the minute or 30 seconds it takes you to get some salt tablets out and consume them is actually going to have some detrimental effect on your running time, which is ridiculous because A, you're not running a road marathon, this is days and days long, and B, you're going to lose much more time if you get dehydrated—you're either going to lose an awful lot of time because you're going to have to have IV fluids, which will lose you hours, or you're going to pull out. So it's better to do what they say, religiously take your salt tablets and manage yourself very carefully.

You're given a road book that describes the stages. It doesn't really make much sense to you unless you're actually well into that sort of thing. It just looks like some topsy-turvy desert picture where you just know it's going to be horrendous. I barely look at it because there's nothing in there that's going to comfort me or relieve me. It's just going to freak me out even more and I'm going to waste precious energy worrying. In my view ignorance is bliss. You'll get your road book and you'll go back to your tent and then all of a sudden you'll hear these sporadic cries of 'Oh God' from other tents when they've read a particularly horrific bit of the road book. All I'm thinking is, *That's just a little bit of energy you've wasted that you're not going to have tomorrow when we've actually got to do it.* So I don't think too far ahead with it.

The general setup of the race is that every stage is a marathon distance, but one stage is a double marathon or beyond, which isn't *too* horrendous in terms of distance, but when you factor in the terrain, the living standards and requirements, the fact that you are carrying everything you need for the whole week (apart from day to day water, which you're given in stages) in a backpack, which weighs about 11 kilos, and the heat, it is appallingly difficult. So you get up in the morning, you prepare yourself meticulously to run each stage. You're constantly worried about losing things. Everything becomes so precious. Every painkiller, every boiled sweet. Everything you've got becomes so precious because you simply cannot replace it anywhere

The whole thing is about 156 miles. It's actually done over six days now, not seven, because they run the last day as a charity stage. So it's about a 156 miles over six days, but the distance varies a bit year to year. You're hoping to do it over five days because the way the format works is Sunday, Monday and Tuesday are roughly marathon distances. Then you have the long stage, around a double marathon distance on Wednesday, and what you hope to do is complete that long stage in one day so that Thursday you get a rest, and then you hit the last marathon on Friday. It used to be Saturday was the last day, with a 15K stage, but they've changed Saturday to a charity stage now so Friday is the last day of the official race. But they have to allow a lot longer than that in terms of race planning, because some people are going to take hours and hours and hours to do the long stage, and some people just aren't. The top Moroccan runners aren't going to take that length of time. They know the terrain. I mean they dance around the dunes, it's completely normal for them, and completely alien for some of the runners.

One year, one guy was struggling but very determined to continue on, and we started the long stage on the Wednesday morning and finished it late Wednesday night or early Thursday morning. There are cut-off times, and if you go beyond those cut-off times you're out of the race. You've got to finish the long stage by late Thursday afternoon. But this poor guy was still out on the course Thursday night. He was still out on the course in the early hours of Friday morning. He walked into the camp just before the next stage started, and the commissaire said to him, 'We've got to pull you out of the race'. He said, 'I'm not pulling out. I want to go on and do the rest'. The commissaire said, 'You've got to pull out. You've overdone the deadline. If you don't pull out, I'm going to have to pull you out'. He said, 'You're going to have to pull me out then'.

They did pull him out, but he'd been out there nearly two days trying to do it. Some people are that focused on finishing, but it really is that hard.

You are in brutal heat; it's 50 degrees plus, and you're not running on a flat surface, you are running in sand. Anybody who's actually tried to run in sand knows how desperately difficult it is. There's a lot of climbing, a lot of agility stuff. It's not just sand dunes, it's jebels. The organisers tend to throw in the unexpected just to make it that little bit more difficult, I think.

You've got your compass to guide you if you get lost, and a flare. I have seen people collapse and be taken to intensive care units in major cities like Casablanca. You witness all sorts of things in that race. I've seen people without a square centimeter of skin on their feet.

Checkpoints are at about every 10 to 12K, and in that time I have experienced a genuine fear that I'm running out of water, because the heat is that extreme. I think the hottest day we've experienced in the desert was just under 55 degrees. So you're running not just in 50-plus degree heat, you're running up sand dunes as high as 800 feet in 50-plus degree heat. Unless you've got this skilled technique that some of the Moroccans have devised over many years to get up some of these sand dunes, you are literally taking one foot forward and falling back three steps. The energy you expend to try and traverse this terrain is quite abysmal.

You're left to your own devices. If you ask for assistance like IV fluid, you get a time penalty. People don't want that. People drive themselves far beyond the point that they can actually come back from. The race is about managing yourself as much as running. I would say the race is at least 50 percent the mental ability to force yourself to keep going when you don't want to force yourself any longer, to the point of pure exhaustion. There is no other way.

Every checkpoint is like an oasis. You focus on these checkpoints like they're five star hotels with bars and swimming pools, when actually all they do is give you a bottle of water and send you on your way. And then you think, *But I'll soon be at the end of the stage.* And then you realise that the end of the stage means this little tiny sanded up place where you can roll out your sleeping bag and do the same thing again, or worse, the next day.

You go through these good patches and bad patches where you kind of yo-yo as runners, somebody might go past you and they look really fresh and then you think, *Okay, that's okay.* Then you'll pass them again in half a mile and they'll look really bad.

I think that race is all about helping others. You are given a very limited water supply, and men and women get the same allocation. As a woman you don't need as much so you're often able to help other runners by sharing what you've got. A lot of people just prefer to wash in it, but I think that's a bit cruel.

Of course, once you hit a problem out there like lacking energy, you've nothing to boost yourself. You've got nothing to say, 'Right, I'm going to have a good old meal. I'm going to have a good old rest, and I'm going to set off tomorrow and it's all going to be new and fresh', because it isn't, because you haven't got anything to rejuvenate yourself with, you've only got what's in your pack, and you've used it probably. So it's tough, and it's kind of disappointing that sometimes people who've got stuff won't share it. You very much see the hoarding side of some people, dare I say it, the nasty side of people, the ruthless side of people comes to the forefront. Where it would be my natural reaction in a situation like that to think, *We're all in it together, let's help each other,* some people's reaction is very clearly, *This is nasty and not a very pleasant place to be, and I don't care about you lot, it's every man for themselves.* You see through the week those reactions that probably don't normally surface come out in people.

CHAPTER 18

Day to Day Misery

IN MDS, EVERY DAY is about a marathon distance, but one day is a double marathon or beyond, which is really tough when you've been doing this repeatedly for three days, and you've been getting back to camp at night. There is nothing at the camp for you apart from this open front open backed tent with a space in it for you to lay your bedroll. There aren't toilets. There aren't showers. There aren't wash facilities. There is nothing. There is a medical tent if you need serious medical intervention. You really hope you don't.

You get all these extra hazards you don't necessarily expect. You could be out there in a sandstorm. We had sandstorms that just blew the whole camp down, literally. They tried to put it back together again but had to just leave it down because it's just so brutal. These are sandstorms where they close in and you can't see anything, you can't stand up, all you can do is get down on the floor and curl up in a ball. There's nothing else you can do. So you're just seeing clothing and bed mats and sleeping bags flying around.

People don't believe me, but in 2012 we got a hailstorm out there. Fortunately I was back at camp with a few others from my tent and we got into the tent. It collapsed on top of us, but the tents are quite thick, so it kind of protected our skin from this appalling battering the hail was giving it. But one poor guy that was also a tent-mate, James, was out on the course during it and he told me a couple of the race commissaires pulled up next to him in this big four-wheel drive, opened the door, and he thought they were going to say, 'Get in. Get shelter', but they just shouted out, 'Are you okay?' Being British, as a natural reaction he said 'Yeah, I'm all right'. And they shut the door and drove off. He came back and his skin was pitted, it was absolutely pitted and scarred where the hail had pummeled him. After that his skin started to fall off his face. He got to a very, very bad point. To try to help him to finish I gave him some antibiotics that I had for emergencies. He took them and he managed to get through, but he finished in a very bad way. I think he was in danger of needing skin grafts.

So with MDS you've got hostile terrain and extreme elements that you're not used to. You've got long distances. You're carting around a big backpack. For most of the participants it's a totally alien climate. It's incredibly hot, indescribably hot, but it can be terribly cold at night. You've only got the food that you've judged that you'll need and that you've carried in your pack. You don't want that big pack to be a single gram heavier than it's got to be, you really don't, because over the course of a week carrying it really starts to tell.

So at the end of day one you get back to the tent and it's damage limitation. And in my case it was an awful lot of damage. Because I had the broken toes, my feet were too swollen to get in my shoes properly.

My right foot was too swollen even before I actually got out there, so by the time the heat had kicked in and the natural swelling you're going to get in those conditions, it was bad on day one.

Your attention to detail on your feet and the management of your feet is absolutely intrinsic to your success in the race. You do not want problems with your feet. You are on them too long in that heat, it's too painful. It's not something I want to experience again.

I also had a problem with my socks. I had decided to wear these socks that were imbued with a sort of metal that deflected heat, to try to mitigate some of the heat from the conditions. A lot of people were wearing them, I'd worn them in training, worn them in my sauna, no problems. But out there I developed an allergic reaction to them, and my whole lower legs just swelled. So I've got the swollen foot, I've got the swollen lower legs. It was all going wrong for me, horribly wrong.

And that was day one. I just could not get my feet in my shoes. I had to modify my shoes and make slits in them. There was nothing else I could do. So the misery continued, until each day you're basically going out there, you're running a marathon, but it's not just about running. It's about climbing, there are rocks, dried up sand, salt lakes—and the heat. It's like the sun's angled to hit you directly. There's no shade, nowhere to stop even at the checkpoints, unless you can get a tiny little space underneath the little tent the race organisers and commissionaires use.

You're not getting any shelter for the whole of the day, so you've really got to be prepared to be a master of your own destiny. And the way you prepared beforehand is basically going to see you through or put you out of the race.

I was fortunate, even though I had the broken toes I was physically very able to complete that race. And it's that *over*-ability to complete the race that allowed me to actually get through it while injured. By day four, which was the long stage, I was traversing the desert—I won't say running because that's a bit of an insult to what we were actually doing—we were getting through it as best we could, me and some of the chaps in my tent. I was probably the strongest of them because it was only my feet that were slowing me down.

We got to a checkpoint and it was dark and the other guys elected to try to get an hour or two of sleep and I didn't want to because I was in a lot of pain, so I was allocated the job of waiting and waking them up. I took the bandages off my right foot to have a look at what the damage was, what was causing me this extreme pain, and I could actually see the bone in my little toe sticking through. I remember thinking, *Oh Lord, this is going to be game over if I do not do something.* I was trying to hide it from people; I didn't want to show the race doctor because I didn't want to be pulled out of the race.

The only thing I had was iodine and I put that on it, which nearly sent me through the roof of the tent. I'd run out of medical tape, so I had to put gaffer tape on them, electrical tape. I didn't have any wadding or padding, so I just put it straight on there. Then it was time to wake the guys up. They were sleeping like little babies in a row, and I did think twice about waking them up to this hell, a sandstorm in the Sahara Desert, and setting them off trudging again when they were physically exhausted. One of the guys, Brett, I don't think he ate after day three, he was so ill. I did have to wrestle with my conscience about waking any of them up into that nightmare. But I woke them. They got up like they were zombies and just set off trudging into the desert like these lost souls wandering around.

I was panicking because there was talk that on the next day there was a river with stagnant water in it that we'd have to get through and if I went through that the next day, what if my feet got infected and I couldn't get through the last stage the day after? And people were like 'Oh no, you'll surely get through the last stage, it's not that long. The last stage is only 15K'. But it's 15 kilometers of the hardest sand dunes in Morocco. So every time your foot moves in your shoe you feel pulling on torn feet.

I really did not want to get them infected. It was just one long panic: Can I get to the finish, can I make this happen? But in the end it turned out the next day was just a straight marathon stage, which is much more my running comfort zone. I think I came quite highly placed in that stage, probably top 10. I did get through the final stage and I did finish. I was in the top two thirds, which was amazing, with the state of my feet; they were all mashed to pieces. But I was quite poorly after.

When I finished, when I got back to the hotel, I wasn't very well because again, you've had this amazing 150-odd miles through the desert. You've got no sanitation. There's no toilets, no nothing there, no showers, no change of clothes. I jokingly say I think I ate a few boiled sweets and a bag full of painkillers. That's basically what got me through. I just couldn't stomach anything, couldn't hold anything down. I think my stomach reacted a bit to the painkillers—or to not taking them anymore, when I got back to the hotel.

But because I finished strong, that's when I decided I'd like to go back the following year and give it a proper hit, a real try at running well in it. And I was quite lucky to be allocated a place for the next year because I'd rescued a lady on the first day.

CHAPTER 19

The Rescue

I WAS IN THE SAME TENT with a lady, Rosie, who was also quite dubious about our circumstances when the reality of what we'd let ourselves in for actually hit, i.e. the heat, the conditions, the struggle. You know, it all sounds very glamorous, 'I'm going to be running for a week in the desert with a backpack and it's this macho man's world that I'm going to get into as a woman'. Reality hits when you arrive. You've got to be extremely tough and prepared to do it and if you can't do it, you will drop out.

Rosie was quite concerned about whether she would be able to cope. Since I had the broken toes, I said, 'Look, let's start together. We'll tread very carefully—literally. We'll see how it goes. We'll get out there and we'll just do what we can'.

I was in trouble with my feet but not with my overall physical ability, but she wasn't doing very well, to the point that she was starting to panic. I think she was thinking this is day one and it's awful and it's going to be awful on day two, day three, and day four is going to be double awful because it's a double length day. So we came to this jebel, a big rocky precipice thing, which you've just got to climb up, get to the top of this ledge-like ridge and run along it. So I'm nattering away, trying to keep our spirits up, and I get to the top and look around and she's nowhere to be seen. I look down the jebel and she's at the bottom, crying. She said, 'I can't go on, I can't go on'.

And in MDS they have what's called a sag wagon. If you're at the back of the race you get picked up and then you're out of the race. In a normal race a sag wagon is a bus. But obviously they can't have a bus in this race, so instead they have a guy with a camel that comes along at the very back to check the stragglers and to make sure that all is okay. That's the official back of the race. And if you're caught by the camel, you're out of the race. So I look into the far distance and I'm thinking, *Oh no, unless my eyes are playing tricks with me, there's a camel*. So we're treading on very dangerous ground here. We had to get up that climb. We had to start upping the pace and hitting it a bit harder than we were.

So I climbed back down and she said, 'I'm packing, I can't go on'. The other one or two people down there were saying something very similar. I told her I'd get her up and she cried that she didn't want to climb. So to get her to the top of the jebel I put her in a fireman's lift and carried her.

This is where people are like 'Oh, so you just happened to know how to do a fireman's lift'. Well yeah, because of the fire brigade. It wasn't just like some impulse, 'Oh I've got to get her from here to here, I'll try carrying her like in the movies', I do know how to do it. Part of training for the fire brigade is you have to be able to climb down a ladder with a body on your shoulder, and it doesn't matter if you're female, you've got to be able to carry an up to fifteen-stone man on your shoulder, up and down a ladder, because if you've got a fire situation and you climb up a ladder and somebody needs bringing down that ladder then you put them on your shoulder and you carry them down. It's part of training and you don't get into the brigade if you can't do that. So I knew how. And Rosie wasn't a fifteen-stone man. She's quite a small lady, so the matter of going down and getting her to the top was not as big of a thing for me as it probably sounds for the average person. It's not like 'Suddenly I came up with this brilliant idea'. It's something that came very naturally to me because of another aspect of my life where it's expected of me to be able to do that. So in that way I was just the right person at the right time.

I climbed that jebel three times. I did it the first time by myself, then left my pack at the top and went back down to carry Rosie up, and then went back for her pack. And it is exhausting. You're expending energy that you haven't got. But, it's that adrenaline situation. You don't think of yourself when there is a real problem going on. And that's where I feel always like yes, I have done this awful race and believe you me, it is awful. It was actually quite a joke to some people, what we are prepared to do to get this little tacky medal. But it isn't like being in a war zone and I don't want to insult other people or animals who are actually in a situation where they can't literally just say, 'Actually, I want to go home' and the response will be 'Okay then we'll get you in a car and you can go back to your hotel'.

It's not like that. Truly, I've seen some people do some wretched things in these races just to save their own skins and ignore anybody else's suffering. That's not me. It's a race. It's something I want to do very desperately for the animals, it's very important to me and I'm very passionate about it, but at the end of the day I'm never going to walk away from suffering, whether it be a human or an animal. I'm never going to ignore that. To put myself first, or my race first, that's not going to happen. When I do road marathons with the Vegan Runners, people I know will sometimes wait at strategic places for me and they'll hand me a bottle of water. And if I'm running with a group I will always offer that water around, and people are always quite surprised by that.

At the end of the day you're racing yourself. I'm not so much racing other competitors, I'm racing myself to do as well as I can for the animals. I'm not interested in doing it to the absolute negation of all that's going on around me and everyone else's suffering. These marathons sound pretty brutal, and they are pretty brutal. But I'm always aware of the suffering that I am trying to address by doing them. The ones that I'm particularly trying to help have no choice. I do have a choice and I am grateful that I have the choice. I'm trying to give them not that choice, but that right, which I've got naturally.

When I arrived back at the top of the jebel with Rosie's pack, I realised that this was not as simple as I thought. She was having some sort of medical problem, hyperventilating. We're at the top of this precipice and all you can see is desert. I knew that I had to get off this ledge in order to find help. They do have vehicles that go around—the big four wheel drives that drive up and down, looking out for people who are in trouble. Something kicked in with me and I thought *I've got to do something. I can't run off and leave her like this.*

So the plan was that I would try to run ahead, get to where there was some sort of civilization, alert them to the problem, get them back to where she was and then set off running again. So I did that. I ran on and I found one of the race officials' cars and got a doctor to come back with me. At that point I knew Rosie was safe and I could run on—had to run on. By this time the camel was approaching and I really did think I was going to get scooped up. So I had to run and get myself sorted out, get my place in the race, which I did do.

I picked up a lot of runners along the way and finished that stage. Got back to the tent. The other guys were back at that time and I remember saying that I was absolutely heartbroken. They were like, 'Oh, Fiona you're back' and I said, 'Yeah, but Rosie's not'.

CHAPTER 20

Reflections

BECAUSE OF THAT SITUATION WITH the rescue I got a place in 2013—with anything going on, word gets around camp, and I had done well towards the latter stages of the race. It was fairly obvious to people that I had this terribly misfortunate thing going on with those broken toes. I desperately wanted to go again, to do the race again and do it well, but it's not that simple, because there is a massive waiting list to do Marathon des Sables, like two or three years. It's on nearly every ultrarunner's list. You've got to have done MDS if you're into ultrarunning. It's the big one. A lot of people from around the world want to do it—or want to say they've done it.

So to get allocated a place the next year was a big thing. Though when I tell people the organisers thought they were giving me something that was very precious, people say, 'Well, if that's like what your friends do for you, what do your enemies do? Ask you to jump off a cliff or something?'

But I did dearly want to be able to go back the next year, in 2013, and do it properly. This time knowing what was expected, knowing what it meant to live out of a pack, knowing what was important and what wasn't important. Stupid things that people might tell you to take, that you don't think of or don't seem very relevant, are actually of utmost importance even though they seem trivial. You're given all this information before you go, which seems nonsensical, but it all falls into place when you get there and you realise that it's so off the spectrum of what you were expecting.

I had a good base preparation the first time, because they do say you need that. You need to have a body that is prepared to run high mileage on a daily basis. But you can't possibly be prepared for it the first time. I was prepared for the high mileage from road running, I can run good road marathon times. I've run good road marathon times but I've never considered myself your archetypal road runner, and when I've spoken to people who are road runners—really top road runners—they've said they wouldn't want to try and transfer over to something like Marathon des Sables. It's very different and I suppose it's like saying something like, 'Well, Usain Bolt is a world-class runner, he could do a marathon'. No, it's a completely different event. It's running, for sure it's running, but it's a completely different style of running in a completely different distance and a completely different set of circumstances, and completely different build, stature, set of muscles that you need to be able to do well.

But the one thing that I did have was an awful lot of base miles, because to get the results I've had in the road marathons, that requires a lot of discipline and a lot of dedication, determination, and actually just going out and doing it. So I had that. That was basically my only preparation. I had to go and purchase this bizarre list of things that you are required to have for these races, and I just couldn't work out what I was supposed to *do* with them.

So I took it as basic as I could. There was a funny incident in the 2012 race when I'd formulated this idea that up until the morning of the race you can have with you what you are prepared to throw away before the race gets going. Somebody had told me to keep a bit of extra food by me the night before the start of the race because if I didn't eat it, I could just throw it away or give it to the Berbers in the morning. And my diet at home is fresh food—a lot of fresh fruit, fresh veg. Obviously I couldn't take that with me in a small pack. But I had kept some fruit by me to have in the morning or the night before so that I could keep my diet as stable and natural for as long as I could. But I must have got a bit jumbled in the morning. I'm getting ready and packing and the first day you wake up in the morning, the tents are ripped down, everybody's really excited and the adrenaline's pumping and there's all this going on. So I must have inadvertently put an apple into my rucksack. And an apple is heavy, when you're weighing everything. I mean, before I left for Morocco Martin had even cut off the wrappers of painkillers to try and make them that little bit lighter—'I've left you a gram there, Fiona'. Great, thanks, one gram less gram to carry.

So that first morning I must've got jumbled in my head as to what I was going to throw away and what I was going to take and pack in my bag. And I put this apple in my bag. And so when we got back to camp that night, after the first day of running, I opened my pack and there was an apple. It was like a mirage. *I've got an apple. Wow.* Everybody else had this horrible, dried, rehydrated, disgusting food, and I've got this apple. I remember biting into it that night when the other guys were hovering over these stoves wondering what to do with this modge that they'd got to eat. And all of a sudden I bite this apple and everybody in the tent looked up. 'An apple, she's got an apple!' It was like mass hysteria over 'Woman Has Apple in Tent'. Headlines around the camp. Brett said to me, 'I knew you were a vegan but I didn't know you were going to—have you got like an apple for every day?' And I'm thinking, *Yes, Brett. That's obviously what I brought in the tiny little pack.*

So preparing for these races is just like 'Do everything as horribly as you can in your training and you won't be far off what it's going to be like in the actual race'. People aren't prepared for the fact that you're not going to have a clean change of clothes every day, because most people come from like civvy street where they'll have fresh lovely running stuff and everything's perfect and clean and they have a lovely long shower when they get home. And I don't actually have that in my daily life, so it's not so much of a shock when I get into the desert. But for a lot of people it is a shock.

Not only are they suddenly running in 50 degree heat, they're running a marathon a day, with a backpack, in hostile terrain. Then there are other things they're not used to, like the food and accommodation situation. I'm not saying I live in an open tent with a bedroll and no toilet or shower, but I think it was a lot less difficult for me than it was for a lot of the people there. Because I live a very physical lifestyle anyway, and a lot of people who want to do these races probably have sedentary work and the only physically active part of their life is the actual running. It's mucky, and I'm used to being covered in mud—or I'm used to not being that comfortable in what I'm doing or quickly changing clothes and just running out there in the middle of the night. So it wasn't so difficult for me in that respect.

There are not really too many ways you can physically prepare for MDS. Some people literally acclimatise by going out to a hot country before the race, but that wasn't a possibility for me. I've got to be at the sanctuary for the animals. But it's very difficult to suddenly go from freezing cold conditions here in England, to the complete other end of the spectrum, 50 degree heat in a desert.

They've got a set list of requirements that you need. You've got to have 2,000 calories a day. Now that doesn't actually sound like a lot, but it means you've got to carry 14,000 calories. It's a lot to carry. At that point you're looking at things that would normally be a big no-no. We walked around the shops beforehand and where a lot of women are going around saying 'How many calories in that? Oh no, I don't want it'. I'm saying, 'How many calories in that, Martin?' and he'd say, 'Oh, 646 in these'. 'Not enough!'

So you've got 14,000 calories, you've got to have a sleeping bag, you've got to have a flare, you've got to carry a giant roll of toilet paper bin liners—if you want to use the toilet in the desert, you've got to do it in a bag—you've got to carry all your medication, your water bottles, your compass. You've got to carry a warm top for night, if you want any change of socks, clothes; you've got to carry tape to tape your feet. Shoes and a cup for drinking out of and a stove and cooking stuff. It's much more basic survival equipment than they usually require for most other desert races. And it's the size—how do you get all that in one pack? Plus most of these packs are designed for men, they're not designed for women. Women who do it tend to have to make do with men's equipment because it's generally men who do this kind of stuff. So it's difficult. You can train with your pack on all day long round here and it's not going to be like setting off in the desert when you're really hot and dirty and tired and frustrated and worried.

When I came home after MDS in 2012, it had beat me up. It took me a long time to get my foot right. I don't lie when I say I could see the bone in the little toe. You will go out to that race and if you're not right, if things are wrong, you're going to lose weight during that race anyway.

You're going to lose a lot of weight. I lost about ten kilos during that week. I wasn't eating and I was expending a lot of energy.

I knew going out there the best possible thing I could hope for was to finish. But I was terribly disappointed I wasn't able to do better, and afterward I decided that the best course of action would be to rest up, recover, and think again about it in 2013, when I could reflect on it, and basically use the promotion that I'd actually done it. Because even though I had not done what I wanted to do in it, people were still interested. There was a lot of interest in it, 'First vegan woman does MDS', kind of thing, so that was positive. I think the *Daily Mail* put me down on a list of 'most inspirational women', because I'd completed this race, I'd traversed this desert to raise funds for the animal sanctuary. So I figured the best way to address this was to go away, recover, and to concentrate on the next year.

CHAPTER 21

A Pull North

MDS 2013 WAS NOT TO BE THOUGH. Not for me at least. In the midst of the time I was taking to recover and train for it, one of the guys with whom I'd done the 2012 race posed me a question. He said, 'You've completed the hottest race on the planet. Why don't you consider doing the Polar marathons next?'

Honestly at first I thought it was a joke, that he was making it up. I asked him what he meant, and he said he meant he thought I should run marathons in the North Pole and Antarctic. And I thought, *Well, there aren't any marathons there.* And then I looked into it and sure enough, there's a marathon at the North Pole, and there's a marathon in the Antarctic.

I had just started training again. It was about late August, early September, and I just literally went out, as normal, running, came back, walked into the house and said, 'Right, Martin, I've got something to tell you'. 'What's that?' 'I want to do these races. I want to do the North Pole

Marathon'. And he just looked at me and, 'Okay, what does that mean?' And I said, 'I don't really know what it means. I've got to find out details'.

Soundbite-wise, if you say to someone, 'I've done a marathon', people know it's extreme. They know that the North Pole is extreme. And it's very common to say, 'Oh, I'm worn out, feel like I've run a marathon', as a way of illustrating that you are tired. Or you come in from the cold and say 'It's freezing out. It's like the North Pole out there'. These are recognised analogies that people associate with toughness. So I was running a very basic calculation through my head. I figured if you put the two together, North Pole and a marathon, you've got a win here. That's definitive, hardcore.

And the marathon is actually at the North Pole. Originally I thought that it would be calling itself the North Pole Marathon, but it would actually just be in a place very far up north in Norway, and there would be a lot of snow and it would be in the Arctic Circle; basically I thought that it would be somewhere *near* the North Pole, but not at the North Pole. It would be on terra firma, at least. But I soon found I was wrong: it takes place on the frozen Arctic ocean at the North Pole.

The only problem was it was extremely, exorbitantly expensive for me, who has to channel all her finance into the sanctuary, to consider entering. So I figured, well it is a goal, but it's a goal for the future because I'm not going to be able to afford it, and it runs at the same time as the Marathon des Sables, it's in April. Obviously, the North Pole Marathon is very restricted in times that it can be run because of access to the Arctic and the North Pole. It's impossible at all about 47 weeks of the year. There's only about five weeks when you can actually get there.

So I figured, okay, that's something to dream about for 2014, get back to the Marathon des Sables training. And then round about Christmas time in 2012 the race organiser, to whom I'd expressed my interest to doing this race, wrote to me and said, 'If you'll consider doing it in 2013, I will give you the place'. And then it was like well, game on. I've got to do it because it's 12,000 euros and I haven't got 12,000 euros, it's a massive opportunity and it might never come again.

So I pulled out of MDS and decided to do the North Pole Marathon and started to train for that. It actually wasn't an awful lot different to training for MDS, because it wasn't going to be a straightforward two hours, 30–40 minute effort. I knew that running at the North Pole was not going to be like a normal race, it was going to be a marathon distance, for sure, it's going to be 26.2 miles, but it wasn't going to be anything like I'd experienced before. Although it's grim training around here, we very rarely get icy snowy conditions. We get hard conditions, but what I have learned is with good body management, sensible planning, and an inherent desire to do this for a reason other than personal reward, you are probably going to be able to be successful.

So one year after running in the 50 degree heat of Morocco, I'd be running in the frigid conditions of the North Pole.

CHAPTER 22

Going North

AROUND CAME APRIL, AND off I went to the North Pole, or as near to the North Pole as they can make it—the closest they can get without the plane going through the ice when it lands. It's got to be very thick, stable ice to land a plane on the Arctic Ocean, otherwise you're going to get a tsunami underneath the ice, and then the plane will go through and it's 13,000 feet of freezing cold water that nobody's going to come and rescue you from.

It is probably one of the most amazing experiences I've ever had, if not the most. You go to a place called Longyearbyen in Norway, which is the northernmost inhabited place in the world. Then you travel in a Russian plane on a four-hour journey to the North Pole. They can't take the whole complement of runners in one go—the plane has to be quite small, it's only got capacity for about 30 or 40 people perhaps, because of the weight landing on ice. They actually use Camp Barneo, the Russian research base that they set up for two or three weeks every year at the North Pole, and that's where you're based for this race.

You fly in and when the plane door opens the reality of the cold hits you. It's beautiful, beautiful, clear sky and all you can see is snow, and you know that you're not even on terra firma. You can hear the ice and the water underneath you cracking.

You're quickly ushered into what are the most phenomenally hot tents you can possibly imagine. It's absolutely baking inside, it's like a sauna. The rationale behind it is at those temperatures your body is just not capable of heating itself gradually. So you come from the cold and you go into hot and that's how you live, in these hot tents. Because it's just so cold outside that you can't balance otherwise.

I was with the first complement of runners that went out there, and was shown to a bunk in a tent. I remember lying there thinking, *This is my address now: Fiona Oakes, care of the North Pole.* I looked out the little plastic window and saw the plane take off and that's it, you're alone. You're at the North Pole, or as close to it as is possible. I don't know what I was thinking at the time. I just kind of laid on my bed, and drifted off into some kind of semi-sleep. And then I was awoken by what I thought was a dog barking. I thought, *Blimey, I'm going delirious now, to add to all my problems, I'm losing my mind.*

But then I thought, *No, that's really a dog barking.* However, it took me about half an hour to get all the gear on that I needed to even venture out the door and have a look and see if there was a dog barking. Sure enough, I went over to the Russian airman who was standing there with this husky dog, and I asked him why he brought a dog here. And he said it was to alert us for polar bears in the area. And I said, stupidly, 'How does he do that?' He said 'he barks'. I thought *Oh, that's good* ... 'But he's barking'. And he said, 'Yes, because polar bears are surrounding the camp'.

To this day, I feel very guilty that I actually encroached on their territory and went to that race. It was something that I did wrestle with beforehand. The only justification I've got perhaps, is that I didn't do it for dinner party conversation and brownie points; not to be able to say 'Look, I've done the most extreme races in the world'—it wasn't about that, and it's never been about that.

I think that if I'd had the recognition I was seeking previously, I wouldn't have sought to go to these extremes. Because my logic behind doing the North Pole Marathon was that if you put these two analogies for toughness together, the North Pole and a marathon, with a vegan woman doing it, surely this has got to address all these issues that I'm so keen to address. Surely this would prove that you are not going to be depleted in any way if you're vegan. If I can run a marathon in the desert, or I can run a 2:38 marathon when I've been on a plant-based diet from a very early age, then surely that's good enough proof that for any sort of lifestyle, this diet is sustainable.

CHAPTER 23

The North Pole

WHEN I ACTUALLY GOT TO THE North Pole Marathon, I found that there have been people who had the opportunity, whether it be financial or just by pure chance, to have treadmills put into industrial freezers to train on, to simulate what it would be like to run in those conditions. Or else they'd been able to go to places with similar conditions to actually train. And I had none of that. And because of my knee, I cannot afford to slip. If I slip, I tear or I dislocate it incredibly easily. There's nothing to keep it stable in there. So I've always veered away from running in icy or slippery conditions. In the desert you don't slip—it's sandy, but you don't actually slip. But on ice you actually do slide, so I didn't really know whether it was going to be possible for me to run in these conditions.

You cannot really simulate running on an ocean. There was a soft covering of snow, which was deep in some places. But what it actually falls on isn't smooth, it's like fractured ice that's then set like that. So you'll be putting your foot through snow and you can't see where your foot's going to land, so you can't judge the angle of your foot. And you might land on anything underneath. There are shots of me running at the North Pole where I'm just literally falling over and getting back up and going on.

I'd no idea what it was going to be like out there. I don't ski, I don't go abroad on skiing trips or anything like that, so I had really no idea of what I was letting myself in for. I took advice as to the buffs and stuff I was going to take. I have to say again, I really, really did not know what to expect. It was this surreal 36 hours of my life going to Longyearbyen. That was an awesome experience in itself, going so far up in Norway, to a set of islands. You get off the plane and it's 'Warning: Polar Bears'. It is extremely bleak, extremely cold. I think it was minus eighteen in Longyearbyen. But we were staying in a hotel there.

There's one plane sitting there, a Russian plane, and that's the one that's going to the North Pole. And the only reason that they've got access to this polar base is that they have an arrangement with the Russians. It's actually a research base that they use. The Russians set it up and I believe the organiser paid to be able to let part of it for this race. The intricacy of setting this base up is quite amazing. You can watch online what they have to do. A soon as the season and the weather permits, they parachute two Russian military officers in there, who go and assess the depth of ice, which is thick enough and near enough to the North Pole to actually set this base up.

Then the Russian military parachute in digging machinery and all the equipment that they need to facilitate this base being erected, the tents. And then it's the Russians that actually set the course up at the North Pole. And it is a fully-fledged course. It's nine laps, just under three miles each. All flagged out. It was surreal, absolutely surreal, with a running gantry. They're very specific on what you can and cannot do in this race. And if you make an error you will come a cropper, no doubt about it. There's the constant danger of hypothermia and frostbite. There's no going back. You've got to be very, very careful out there.

They set up a few tents with bunks and when you arrive you're shown to one. You can't take hardly any luggage with you. You can take a bag but you're not going to be there for long. You don't want loads of accoutrements. You want a few basic things and that's it. It's going to be in and out to do this race. But logistically it takes them a long time to actually get all of the runners there, so you have to have a few personal things, but you don't have spare running gear, not beyond spare headgear. I went into this tent and was shocked. I thought I was going to need warm-weather stuff. I didn't think I was going to have to take everything off but my T-shirt, because I was sweating. I didn't want to sweat, because those were the only undergarments I had to run in, and I didn't want to have them wet from sweating in the tent and then go outside into the cold, because that was just going to be potential disaster. So I stripped down to this T-shirt while I was waiting for the plane to fly back to Longyearbyen to refuel and get the rest of the runners out there. It was about eight hours we were left waiting for the other runners to come back, so they could think about setting up the course and get us off running.

I tend to think, 'All marathons start at 9 a.m.' But obviously at the North Pole they don't. It's 24-hour sunlight at that time of year, and they're not going to close the roads because there aren't any. There's no spectators, nothing else to think about but the race, getting it off. I think we started running about half past midnight.

I was absolutely horrified when I got out and I saw what I had to do. I thought, *Oh, I'm not going to be able to do this. I'm just not going to be able to do it.*

I think I took four hours 50 to do that race. Some of the other runners were taking 12 hours, if they were finishing. But you're not running for four hours and 50 minutes, or 12 hours, or whatever your time may be. You have to keep stopping during the race. You have to stop, come off the course, walk very slowly because it's icy, into the hot tent where you can then do things like have some boiling water if you need it to warm yourself up. You can take a gel. You can change your glasses, because some people's eyeglasses were shattering in the cold. You need to see where you're going but you really do need your eye cover. But then you're getting condensation in your glasses.

If you go out on a lap and you've misjudged it, there is nothing out there that's going to help you for that three miles. And it's not three miles equals 18 minutes, as it does on the road. Three miles can equal an awfully long time. And it's not just about running. If you blow up during a road marathon, you simply do not finish, or you get a slower time. If you blow up out there, it could be a disaster. A real disaster. We're not talking about running a bit slower. You are risking what could be very long-term health problems if you get it wrong out there.

There is nobody to come and pick you up. There's no nutrition. You can't carry a gel or a sweet or anything with you. I did actually have a treat—my treat for the race was a couple of boiled sweets in my pocket that I thought, *If all gets very desperate, I will resort to having one of these.* I hadn't even taken anything to have for each lap. I figured that for that length of time I probably wouldn't need too much and I wouldn't be running that fast. So I thought I might just have something almost not for nutritional purposes, but to divert my attention, to give me something else to focus on.

So I'm running along about halfway through, and I decided to go to Plan: Boiled Sweet. But when I actually fished in my pocket I couldn't find it. I thought, *But I'm sure I put my boiled sweet in my pocket.* And then I realised in light of the fact that it was much colder than an industrial freezer, it had crumbled and gone to nothing.

I came in after a lap and I needed to change my head buff, but I couldn't get it off. I tried and tried and couldn't do it. In the end one of the Russian guys had to cut it off me with a big pair of scissors, because it had frozen so solid and part of it was frozen to my hair, and we had to cut that off as well. It was all entangled in it because I had long hair. The condensation from your breathing makes it wet, because your face is completely enclosed. Because you just don't want any part of you to get exposed to that kind of climate. So you get condensation and then it freezes. Then I had to put a change of headgear on and go out again. So my point is you're not running for that length of time. You're actually administering to yourself for a lot of that time.

I'd realised very soon into the race that the important thing was to be able to maintain a pace, to not slow down, to not allow your body temperature to drop, because then you're going to get hypothermia. When I actually finished the race I was absolutely elated. Not at winning the race, not at anything more than the fact that I'd got through this awesome achievement of surviving out there for that length of time and been able to do what I'd done for that length of time and being, as far as I was concerned, in one piece. Because I will say I was frightened while I was out running. I started to have panic attacks at some point and think, *What if I've gone too quickly? What if I get cold, what if?*

I ran up to the finish, and I've got my little teddy out, I was ready with Percy. I got to the finish line and there was no one there. No one there to take any photos or anything. It's the North Pole Marathon finish and I won it, and no one was there. So I finish and I go into the hot tent and they were sitting there, all the race organisers and photographers, drinking hot drinks. They looked up at me as if to say, 'Hello, what are you doing here?' like I had just come in from the shops, and I said, 'Well, uh, I've finished'. 'Oh have you? We didn't realise, we thought you've got another lap to do'. 'No, I've actually—', 'Oh yeah gosh, you've finished'. And by this time I was cooling down. And then they said to me, 'Can you go back out, run about 800 meters away and come up to the finish line again, and we'll photograph you?'

It was not the first thing I felt like doing, I'll tell you that. But I did it. I felt a responsibility, I was grateful of the place that I had been given there, I wanted to do everything right. So I did it and didn't say anything about it, but it was a bit of a tough ask. This ultimate relief of coming to the finish line and being able to get out of this bit of hell and then to be shoved back into it again. The reward of finishing was basically go out there and get back on the course.

I set a record, the fastest woman to ever run a marathon at the North Pole, and that was a course record by absolute miles. I placed on the podium with the men, I did everything I could've hoped for.

And you only have to look at how some of the other participants fared to get an idea of what those conditions were like. A guy in my tent got hypothermia. His name was Jeremy, and he'd gone out there with his father, who was running, and his mother, who'd come to watch them. I saw Jeremy before the race and he was a great big strapping lad, he looked very much like Prince Harry. It was that kind of build, very athletic.

I came back in after I'd won my race and found Jeremy with his mother and the doctor that we had taken with us to administer to the runners. I asked Jeremy's mother what was wrong, and she said he'd got hypothermia. What had happened was he'd stopped for a toilet break. I can't emphasise enough in this race the cold at the North Pole. It's beyond brutal. You're in this position where you're in these uber hot tents where you can't wear much at all. You're just sweating. But to go outside it takes you nearly a half hour to get all the gear on, and you can't just pop out and pop back in because the little toilet shed that they dig (which is a hole just away from camp), it's just like 25 meters, but it seems like the other end of the earth. You can't just run out to it and run back because the cold is the kind of cold that you throw some water up in the air and it freezes. You're constantly looking around you. You're looking at everybody's faces. Have they got white spots? Anybody that gets a white spot, you tell them, 'You're getting frostbite'. It's very, very important to manage yourselves there.

I asked Jeremy's mother what they were going to do, and she said she really didn't know what to do. Her husband was out on the course still going around and Jeremy was there in the tent and she didn't know whom she needed to be with. And because Jeremy was in my tent, I said, 'Look, I'll look after Jeremy, I'll keep an eye on him. He won't leave my sight. I'm not going anywhere. I'm in the opposite bunk. You go and look after your husband and he'll be safe with me'. We got him back to the hot tent, our bunk tent, and honestly I've never seen anyone in that state. Shaking to the point of rocking his bunk. It really brought it home to me, because he was young and fit, a strapping great lad, and he'd succumbed to this terrible cold.

There were other instances on the course. This one guy said he stopped on course for a toilet break, and when he tried to get running again, he simply couldn't move. He thought his muscles were paralyzed. But then he realised that because he had sweat on his clothing, in the time it took him to do what he had to do, his clothes had frozen. They were like a suit of armor he couldn't run in.

Another guy, Pedro, he nearly lost his ear to frostbite. Another guy got hypothermia, though not so bad as Jeremy. But he decided it was damage limitation time. His tactic was to come back into the tent, spend an hour resting and warming up, and then go back out onto the course and finish his race. But I was very lucky. I didn't really have too many problems in that department—at one point I felt some goings-on with my big toe on my right foot, and I thought, *Oh, no! Is this the start of frostbite?* But fortunately it wasn't. I came away unscathed from that race, which I thought was an absolute testament to what I believe in and the way I live my life. But these were all stories that are coming up after the race because when you're there you're not chatting to people. People come back to the tent absolutely depleted of energy. It's kind of surreal. People are numbed by the experience, the awesomeness of the experience, getting through it and being glad it's over.

CHAPTER 24

Coverage

When I came home from the North Pole race there was an awful lot of positivity. I thought I'd achieved what I wanted to do. The BBC rang immediately. I got home and they said, 'We've heard you've broken a record in this polar race. Can you come up to Salford and speak about the experience?' They said they'd pay my expenses (which is a big thing for me), said I could bring my mum, that's fine, they'd get me a hotel. They said they wanted me to open and close BBC Breakfast. And then the researcher said, 'There's just one thing—we would prefer it if you didn't mention the fact that you're vegan'. And I thought, *But that's the whole point of me being there—that's the punchline.*

I have noticed this on other occasions. In 2012 when I'd done the Marathon des Sables, there was an article written in the *Daily Mail*, and I was voted one of their most inspirational women of the year. You know, 'Woman runs across desert to save her animals' story, but at no point in the article did they mention the fact that I was vegan. And I've always had the impression that that's the barrier. That's the barrier to getting my athletic achievements out there. It's because as far as they're concerned, I've done it with a hidden agenda. I've done it to promote something that they're not happy to promote.

I went up to the BBC, I sat on the sofa there live and the whole time that they were talking and questioning me I was thinking, *How do I mention the fact that—Dare I? Dare I? I better not. What do I do? How do I do it? How do I say it?* You can't just suddenly sort of start chatting about the weather and then blurt out 'Oh by the way I'm vegan', you can't do that.

You're only as good as an interviewer will allow you to be, and they very much lead these questions and answers, and in the end they asked me why I'd done it, why I'd run a marathon at the North Pole. And I think if I'd said, 'Because I'm an adrenaline junkie and I just wanted to do it because it was there', I think they could have connected with that a lot better than the answer I gave. Which was that I'm an honorary patron of the Vegan Society and it was the 70th anniversary the following year and I wanted to do something to celebrate that, so I decided I would go and try and run this race ... which I've won, and I broke the course record and I placed with the men and I've done really well.

There was no uptake on it whatsoever. The second part of the interview came later in the show and there was no uptake on this vegan diet. No, 'Oh, that's very unusual', or 'People might not think you can do that on a plant-based diet'. There was nothing. It was just like dead silence and *Let's just ignore the fact that she said that and move on to the next question.* Which was quite hurtful, but I've become quite resilient to it now. It's almost what I expect. They didn't want it on there.

CHAPTER 25

An Around-the-World World Record

THAT'S WHEN THE WORLD record attempt first came up.

A lot of the guys from the North Pole race were encouraging me to do this world record for the fastest woman to go to every continent and the North Pole and run a marathon. I'd had no idea that record existed. I used to think you drop off the end of the world if you run past 26.2 miles on a road; it never even occurred to me that there were all these strange weird wonderful exotic races in other parts of the world. But it turns out yes, there was a record to be the fastest woman—in days—to actually do a marathon on every continent, plus the North Pole. Obviously, there is only one marathon at the North Pole. So if you're going to do it, that's your benchmark. You cram all of your other races into this period of time and you end up in the Antarctic in November and complete that marathon.

It was a lot to take in; and then there was the not unimportant question of was I even physically capable of attempting this record. But when I'm training for marathons, I'm running a marathon distance every Sunday, plus probably 70 or 75 miles during the week as well. I've been running many times the distance of a marathon in the course of a week. So I figured that yes, I could do this world record attempt because basically it's what I do every Sunday. And weighing on my decision was the fact that I was already entered in the Antarctic race.

So I came back from the North Pole in April, riding high on the wave of initial media interest. I thought the world record attempt was a good idea and I wanted to do it. But then, when things die down and you look at the logistics of actually getting yourself to every continent, in a relatively short space of time—the financial side of it and the physical side of it—it just wasn't going to happen. The sanctuary is what is most important. Keeping the sanctuary going financially is tremendously important to us. Martin's salary was paying for the vast majority of the sanctuary funds that we needed, he's only got his 25 holiday days off and his work was not going to allow him time off work to cover me so I could go to every continent at my leisure and run a marathon. It just wasn't going to happen.

The only way I would be able to do it was make flying visits to each continent, run a marathon, fly back home, be there while Martin went to work, then head out to the next continent on the weekend. I looked into it and I thought, no, this is not going to go anywhere. This is just a no go. I won't say I forgot it, but I got embroiled in other things, with the sanctuary, with a lot of other things in my life. But the thought of it was always there, niggling away at the back of my mind. I couldn't forget it, and at the beginning of August I thought *This is just too good to miss.* I couldn't pass this up. This is an opportunity of getting in the Guinness Book of World Records as a vegan...and I'm throwing it away. And I knew I was throwing it away because there was no way I was going to go back to the North Pole and run that marathon again.

So, I explored the potential costs. No way we could afford it. So again, I went to my parents and I explained, and my mum in particular knew that it had been preying on my mind. She said, 'Look, the only thing I can suggest is that we remortgage our cottage and then we can raise some funds and you can do it'. And they were looking into doing that. But in the meantime I'd written to one or two people to ask for help, and a guy from America had actually written back to me and said he'd like to support it. He didn't want anything back from it, didn't want any publicity, didn't have a business, just wanted to promote veganism. That's all he wanted. He thought this was an excellent way of doing it, and advised I go ahead. So then it was on.

But by then I'd left myself very, very, short for races that I could actually get to in time. People think that I was actually going to each continent and then leaving that continent to go to the next, like I was leaving Australia and then going to Africa. It wasn't that at all, I couldn't do that; literally I haven't got the days to go from continent to continent like that. So for instance I went to Australia and back in less than four days: went there, ran a marathon, came home, and the minute I got home within half an hour Martin was on his way to work.

The whole thing was difficult to organise. You can't just say 'I've been to every continent and done a marathon. Here's the world record, you endorse it, Guinness'. You can't just do that. You have to tell the Guinness Book of World Records what you're intending to do, where you're intending to do it and you have to provide a lot of proof that you've actually done it.

The one thing that actually worked for me, and I'm very fortunate about, is that the first race I ran, I won. I didn't intend to, I just thought, I've got to take this uber steady because I've got to keep churning this effort out, with all of this enormous amount of travel every couple of weeks, so I've got to take this really, really steady. So I selected a marathon in Europe as my first leg. I thought I'd better check that I could actually do this marathon and then I can get the European one under my belt for free, so to speak. I did it in the UK, in the Isle of Man. But then I ran a relatively quick time, and I won it. I ran what they call a championship-qualifying time for London Marathon, which is the benchmark in this country of a fast marathon for a woman, and it gives you an automatic entry into the London Marathon. Which is a really rare opportunity because of the big waiting list and the big ballot vote. People get knocked back for London a lot. But this gives you an automatic entry, qualifies you for the next two years.

So I got home and Martin said to me, 'You do realise that if you could do that in every race, you would get two world records instead of one: Set aside the days it takes you, you'd be the fastest woman in running time; you'd be the quickest to actually physically run them not just logistically but in actual ability, to run a marathon on every continent and the North Pole'.

And so that first race I set the benchmark a hell of a lot higher, because not only did I need to go to every continent and run a marathon on each of them, I now had to churn out these really, really, quick times every week on those different continents. I couldn't just amble around these races. My goal now was to run them and do as well as I could in them, and get a decent time in each, so when the accumulated times were added all together, I would be the fastest woman ever to have actually physically run on all these continents.

So I decided to plow on. The next race was in Australia. That one was a big ask, because we had to go to Australia for the weekend basically, from the UK. We had to go there and back in four days. It's almost a 24-hour flight to Australia, to Adelaide; tip out the plane, turn up on the race start, run the marathon, place in the marathon, do the championship time, get back on the plane, come home so that immediately after I arrived Martin could go to work, to cut down the amount of days off he had to take to facilitate me doing this.

We were in Australia less time than we were flying there. I remember arriving through customs with just this tiny hand luggage and the bloke was kind of looking at our entry visa and saying, 'Is this correct? Are you going on to like New Zealand or somewhere?' No, no. We're going home. He said, 'You're going home tomorrow?' I said, 'Yes, I'm going home tomorrow'. And he said, 'So you're in Australia, on a day trip from the UK?' And I thought about it and I thought, oh my Lord, I suppose this sounds a bit suspicious. I've flown all this way just for the day. I said, 'Oh yes, yes, but don't worry, I've got a reason for being here'. And he said, 'Oh, what's that?' And I said, 'I'm running a marathon in the morning'. And he just looked absolutely gobsmacked. He said, 'Well, I pity you with jet lag'.

But the funny thing is, I didn't get any. I don't think I was gone long enough to actually have time to get it. Because I placed in the marathon; I did exactly as I set out to do, came home, Martin went to work that afternoon, the next day I was unwrapping the bread for the animals, business as usual. Now I had to get ready for the next race.

The next race was in far Russia; Omsk, in Siberia. In fact the Omsk International Marathon is the biggest race in Russia. The most recognised marathon. So I trundled off there a week or two later and did exactly the same thing in that race. Placed in it and came back with the time that I needed to run. Every time I ran these quicker times, the pressure was then on to keep doing it, to get these two world records instead of the one world record that I'd originally set out to do.

The travel to Siberia was really laborious and you were thrown forward in time. So I arrived and I'd had no sleep and I had a day to recover there and then tip out and run. It was a very competitive marathon and it was quite tough. And of course you do get tired when you've been travelling, and then suddenly you've got to run and the pressure is on.

Each subsequent race was more pressure, because you realise this really is game on now. I've got these ones banked, I've got three marathons, I've got four marathons, I've got five marathons banked. You really don't want to make an error. But you're getting more and more tired and more and more prone to injury and fatigue, and illness as well. All that flying and the kind of things you pick up on planes. You get extremely stressed out, because you've only got one chance and if something goes wrong, the whole thing is out the window. There was a lot of support for me doing it, but a lot of financial pressures for me to do it. Because obviously it was a big investment for my sponsor, and I didn't want to let him down, I didn't want to let the animals down, didn't want to let anybody down.

So I went off to Omsk and did that race. And I did a big press conference in Russia. I tried to use every race for as much benefit as I could for the animals, and when I'd arrived in Omsk, exhausted, there was a call to my bedroom and it was a girl who was desperate for me to try to help this dog sanctuary in Omsk. She said any positivity I could get for them by being there would be so much appreciated. So I went out there that evening. She picked me up, took me out to the sanctuary, I met the lady who runs it and I gave her all the dollars I'd got with me, US dollars, to help the sanctuary. I hadn't got very much. And she said, the biggest thing you could do if you have any opportunity, is to mention us to the press and media.

At the press conference for the race later, nobody asked any of the professional runners any questions, even though they had quite good runners there. All of the questions were directed to me. I felt kind of embarrassed, sitting there along Kenyans, Ethiopians, top runners, and me at the end. I bet the others were thinking, 'Who is this person at the end they keep asking all the questions to?' But I managed to say that I'd come out there specifically to raise awareness for the sanctuary. And at the end of the race, the people from the sanctuary were all there to meet me. It was so moving. It was a beautiful experience.

The next challenge was to go to the US and run a marathon for North America. I'd been asked by Chicago to go and it was that weekend, but I veered away from the Chicago Marathon because there is a bit of a media frenzy around these races and I literally needed to be able to get in and out to a race as quickly as possible. It's very stressful in big city marathons simply to get to the race start. It's a bit of a circus, it really is. So I'd elected to do the nearest one I could find on the East Coast, which was the Atlantic City Marathon. So I went out there, and I remember it was a horrible day. The wind off the Atlantic was absolutely ferocious. They immediately said at the technical meeting, do not run on the boardwalk because it is treacherous and you will slip. And the one thing I did not want to do was slip. I really didn't want to tear anything in my knee. So I set off very gingerly.

I think I won that race. I was trying to help some of the guys in there. This young guy, he was a really kind, chatty guy and I was literally just trying to get around as best I could. It was very windy. I was kind of tired for that race, and he desperately wanted to bust a marathon qualifier. And I'm never sure what the qualifiers are, I don't know at my fingertips what each elite-qualifying standard is. He said he needed to run 3:10 or under. And I said, well stick with me, we'll try and do it together, we'll take some of the windchill off each other. He was absolutely desperate. He wanted his place in Boston. And I was running with him for quite a long way, and unfortunately he got fatigued in the last few miles. I said, just try and hang with me, get behind me, do whatever you've got to do and I'll just keep knocking out this pace.

And I felt really sad actually when I got to the finish line because I'd run the time he wanted to run. If I could have given him the time for the sake of the few minutes that it had cost him, I would've done. He was absolutely bereft, and that always stuck with me. I was quite on a high, because I got through it, and I got through it well. Better than I ever expected. And he hadn't and that made me feel really sad.

But then it was back on the plane and back home. And there was a little bit of a wobble. Because that Sunday night, we went straight to the airport to come home after the race and I said to my mum, 'I don't feel so good'. It was only about a seven-hour flight or so, but during that time I just felt myself getting worse and worse and worse. I'd got some sort of cold or flu thing going on, but I got off the plane and I was sick, sick, sick. It didn't help that we'd booked a taxi to meet us and get us home so that Martin could go to work, and the taxi didn't come. So we're stuck at Heathrow, wondering what to do. We couldn't just get in any old cab because it was going to be too expensive, because it's quite a long way from Heathrow to where we live.

By the time we arrived home I was quite poorly and I remember just ticking off days. I had about 12 days before I had to go Africa and run the African leg, and I just wasn't getting any better.

Even when we went, we had a heck of a journey getting back to Heathrow, on the Friday before the race, which was to be on Sunday morning. We were stuck in traffic for six hours, we nearly missed the flight out, and it was the last flight I could possibly take to get registered for the race and run it on Sunday morning. It was tremendously stressful. At that point, when we were stuck on the M25 with no traffic going anywhere, engines turned off, massive tailbacks, no way—we thought—we were going to make this plane, I thought, *Let's just go home. I just can't do it.* I felt so dreadful.

In the end we did catch the plane, somehow, and we arrived at the airport in Casablanca, my mum and I, and nobody spoke the language, it was really late at night and there was no taxi. I thought, *What are we going to do? We're stuck here.* We couldn't get out of the airport to go and see if the taxi was outside because then they wouldn't let you back in. And we couldn't argue because we couldn't speak the language anyway.

Then I suddenly clocked out the corner of my eye a guy chatting on his telephone and from his physique and the snippets of his conversation I could catch, it seemed like he was probably going to run the marathon and had also been left in the same position. So I kind of latched onto him—his name was Ian and I've stayed in touch with him since then—and he helped us and we got to the hotel and we muddled our way to the race registration and muddled our way on to the race start.

I really did surprise myself in that race, because with my illness I thought I'd be struggling to finish and I certainly would not be able to run the time I wanted to run. I thought it would take me forever, and I certainly would not place. I thought it would just be so horrendous, I didn't know what to do. And of course it was extremely hot as well. It wasn't the most organised of races, but apparently it is the best one to do this challenge in Africa, because it's only just considered to be in Africa and quite easy for me to get to. It was a hard race for many reasons, one of which was there wasn't a great acceptance of women who were actually running the race.

I don't know how I got through it, but I did—I placed in it and I did the time I wanted to do in it. So then it was back home to the UK to try to recover and gather myself to do the last two marathons in this series, which were going to be the South American leg and the Antarctic leg.

CHAPTER 26

The Volcano Marathon

I HAVE TO SAY, IF I'D HAVE known what I was letting myself in for with the South American and Antarctic legs, I question whether I would have actually gone. It was so horrible. And I'm forever grateful that my mum actually went with me and witnessed it, because if she hadn't I don't think she would have believed it. I got through it. That's the main thing, I did get through it. If I'd just been trying to do this world record attempt for myself though, I wouldn't have done it, I wouldn't have put myself through it. But I wasn't doing it for myself, so I did.

The validation for Guinness World Records is quite strict. You can't just turn up with a Garmin and say, 'Look, I've run these marathons, give me a world record'. It's not like that at all. You have to be super well authorised throughout it. Every race has got to be rubber stamped that, yes, not only has a person called Fiona Oakes run these races, you've got to prove it's you. Because when you think about it, you could stick

someone into a race, enter them as you, and there isn't going to be a lot of debate from the race organisers as to whether it is you or not. And the Antarctic and South American races are very expensive, time consuming, and laborious to get to from the UK. To combine the time, the expense and the logistics necessary, I decided to run the South American leg and then five days later go down to Antarctica. So you're committed, more than you would be with a more run-of-the-mill race.

The problem was the race I had to do in Chile was at 14,400 feet altitude on a volcano. If you've ever tried to run or even walk at 14,400 feet altitude up the side of a volcano, you know it's not the best place to be when trying to produce a quick marathon time.

I'd entered this race in the Atacama Desert, called the Volcano Marathon, and I'd convinced myself that it wouldn't be too bad running a marathon at 14,000 feet altitude—and above—and I really hadn't given it that much thought. Until about three weeks before leaving for the race, I went to the dentist and mentioned what I was going to be doing and he looks at me a little bit suspiciously. 'So ... so you're familiar with altitude, are you?' he asked. 'No, no, not particularly', I said, 'but I'm pretty fit, so I should be able to get through it, I think'. He said, 'Well, you do know it's not actually always to do with how fit you are, right?' The alarm bells started to go off in my mind and I asked, 'What do you mean?' And he said, 'Well, some people just can't cope at altitude'. He said, 'For instance, my wife and I went on a trekking holiday and it was at 8,000 feet in Peru and we just couldn't cope'. He in particular couldn't cope so he had to come down. They couldn't manage. He said, 'I am very experienced and I just couldn't stand it. My body would not cope with it'. I thought, *No. No. No. Not only am I going, I'm taking my mum as well. What is this going to be like? It's going to be dreadful. It's going to be horrendous. We're going to be coming back in a couple of boxes if we're not careful.* And it *was* brutal.

We went to Santiago in Chile and then we flew to Calama, and then drove on to San Pedro. I arrived and one of the other runners came out and said, 'Did you hear what happened?' And I asked, 'What? What?' He said, 'This runner got off the plane, he came here, and he was so ill in San Pedro,' (which is about 10,000 feet), 'he had to go home. He couldn't even cope with being here'. I thought, *Oh, God.* The race was in a couple of days. We'd done a little bit of trial running in the desert, but nothing like 26 miles.

The morning of the race came and they drove us to where they were going to hold the race, at 14,400 feet. It's the highest average altitude race ever held, apparently. It's tough, and you're not running on a flat road. You've got to contend with the fact that you're 'running' at altitude, but you're not actually running. You are battling terrible terrain. It was on volcanic sulphur and the climbs were completely brutal.

You had to be like a mountain goat. Nothing survives up there. There is no vegetation, there's very little wildlife. One guy from Al Jazeera TV was doing it. It had been his intention to do that race, which was being filmed, and then go down to Antarctica and do the race there. He pulled out at 30K and said it was just lunacy. He said he wasn't doing it because if he did do it, he wouldn't be able to run the main prize, the race in Antarctica. There was no way he could do both of them. His film crew were in a state—one girl, who was only in her 20s, she just couldn't handle the altitude. I asked one of the race organisers what do you do if you can't cope? and he said, 'There's nothing you can do but come down and get oxygen'. There was no way of going back. And I thought, *Oops. This is going to be a really hard day at the office.* It was.

They got Mohamad Ahansal out there, a multiple Marathon de Sables winner, and I was running with him and a guy called Basti Haag, from the clothing company UVU, and we were running together quite well until, at about 28K, I rolled my knee. I'm not sure how it happened exactly, if I stepped on an unstable stone or something, I don't actually know what it was. I just rolled my knee and slipped and I knew I'd damaged it badly the minute that I did.

Basti would've stayed with me, but I told him to go on, since there wasn't anything he could do. The race commissaires came over to me and it was swelling in front of their eyes, but I didn't ever think about pulling out. I just thought, *Okay, I'm going to have to walk. I'm going to have to do what I've got to do to finish and it's not going to be pretty.* And it really wasn't. It was really tough and if you've never been at altitude, the kind of tough that it was is very hard to explain.

For instance, your fingers swell, your feet swell to direct the blood supply to the most important organs of your body. The rest of it just shuts down. Your brain feels like it's going to explode. The pumping in your head, the banging, you want to just rip it out. It's brutal and no matter what you do, you can't do anything about it. You can't raise your game. There is literally nothing you can do and no one around to help you. I was almost delirious.

But when I came across the finish line, I was actually in the top placing of the runners. I think purely because I'd got so far running quickly in the first part, I'd only had to go on another 14K in that state, and some people were in that state literally from the word go.

There were two buses going back to San Pedro. All I could think about was being on the first bus—finishing quickly enough to be on the first bus and getting my mum out of there too, because I was scared. It was a scary experience.

But I got across the finish line. Then there was one doctor there that wasn't being very helpful, and it was because of Basti that I actually got some help. Basti used to be a vet before he went into this clothing business, and he spoke Spanish, and he insisted that I get some IV pain relief. I remember lying in the back of this ambulance at 14,400 feet up the side of a volcano in the Atacama Desert thinking, *How the hell am I going to recover from this? The doctor has just told me that I am not going to run again this year.* It was November 14th. *How the hell am I going to run in Antarctica in five days and get round and do this world record? How am I going to do that? That's not going to be possible.* I was absolutely bereft.

I couldn't even tell Martin what had happened, I remember just sending a photograph home of me in the back of an ambulance with this IV fluid going in my arm and my leg just huge. I didn't know what to do. We did get on the first bus. We had to wait a long time to go, for enough runners to come to fill this first mini bus so we could actually go. Then it was a hundred kilometers back to San Pedro and I just sat there trying not to think. The other runners were stupefied by what they'd gone through. It was just horrendous. Just complete silence in the bus. I couldn't even bend my leg. We got back to the hotel, Mum and I, and we just went back to our room. It was an awful, awful time and we had no idea who to turn to. We were stuck, literally, in the middle of nowhere, without a plan. It was a pretty low point of the whole mission, so to speak.

We got into Santiago and I was pretty much panicking. Looking at the boards that come up for the airlines thinking, *That one's going back to London. I wish I was on it.*

I shuffled off to go and get mum and myself a drink, and when I was in the queue I got talking to a guy who was an airline pilot. He asked me what I was doing there and I told him I'd been in the Atacama Desert. And he's like, 'That's great. Were you stargazing, or...' And I tell him 'No, no. I've been running a marathon'. And he said, 'You've been running a marathon in the Atacama?'

'Yeah'.

147

He said, 'That's real high altitude'.

'Yeah. The one we ran was at 14,400 feet'.

And he looked at me like *you crazy person*. He said, 'We can fly that low. You shouldn't be running a marathon at that kind of altitude. That's dangerous. That's really dangerous'.

I said, 'I know, I've learned my lesson there'.

But that kind of brought it home to me, and I'm feeling really low as I'm taking these two coffees back, and then all of a sudden in the queue to get on the plane to go down to Punta Arenas, the city you fly out of when you're going to Antarctica, I just could hear all these exuberant, excited voices of people who had arrived from other places, their home countries, to go to the Antarctic race. They're all full of excitement and joy, *We're going to Antarctica!* and I'm full of dread and horror. I've hurt my knee, I've got these world records hanging over me and I'm dicing with whether I can do them or not. I've failed, basically, and all these people are so excited about this upcoming race, and I'm just thinking, *Oh, I wish it would just go away or be cancelled or something.* Thinking what to do when we get to Punta Arenas, and what exactly my plan was going to be when I got to Antarctica, if I got there at all.

We were going to go to our hotel room and just hide away, but now it was Plan 'Trudge round Punta Arenas on a drab Sunday afternoon and look for walking poles and walking boots, because I sure as heck can't run in Antarctica'. We did manage to purchase some individual walking poles and some walking boots, and the plan was to go to Antarctica and just set off and trudge round, trek round, limp round, whatever I had to do to finish the last marathon. Mum would be staying in Punta Arenas.

Then there was the question of whether we would either fly out that Monday night or the very early hours of Tuesday morning. It was that much to the wire that they said we were to go back to our hotel rooms on Monday and wait for a call, and the call would either be to say, 'Get your gear, we're flying tonight' or, 'We'll be flying in the morning, early'. Mum and I laid in that room and worried. The whole time I was thinking *I've got another hour to recover my knee. I've got another hour.* Any time I had to recover, it was so precious, and when that call came through the guy said to me, 'I've got some bad news'. And I just thought, *Oh, no, we're going today.* He said, 'We've got a flight in the morning'. So I had another few hours to rest in a bed with my leg, which desperately needed all the rest it could get. So the next morning I acted on instruction, I got to the race hotel where they were going to transfer us to the airport in the very early hours, and we went off to Antarctica.

CHAPTER 27

The Antarctic Ice Marathon

THE STORY WITH THE ANTARCTIC Ice Marathon is that you go right deep into Antarctica, about halfway into the center of Antarctica, and there is this camp called Union Glacier. You fly over the ocean, over half of Antarctica and land at this camp. It's nestled behind some mountains, a spectacular place to land. Big four-wheel drive trucks pick you up and they shuttle you from the airstrip down to a basic but adequate camp, which is used for all sorts of Arctic expeditions. Absolutely surreal, awesome experience.

When I was down there an Arctic explorer called Richard Parks was there waiting to set off on a solo, unassisted trek to the South Pole. It's quite a hub. We arrived at camp and the plan was that there would be a marathon the following day and there would be a 100K the day after, and then we would leave the day after that, on the Saturday. But flying to

Antarctica is tremendously difficult because the weather has to be balanced precisely right.

We flew in from southern Chile, Punta Arenas, and the weather there is unpredictable. They suffer a lot with wind down there, gale force winds. So taking off and landing is difficult for a plane. There is absolutely no way that a plane will be allowed to fly to Antarctica if it's not guaranteed to be able to land, unload, reload and get out of there. I learned this from a pilot who spent his life shuttling between the two poles doing reconnaissance missions and taking in supplies. He explained that in those kind of freezing temperatures a plane can't be down for very long. They did actually have one stuck there for two years once because it stayed on the ground too long, there was absolutely no way they could get it back in the air. So it's very important that when you fly in you're able to fly out again.

So we arrived, we unloaded, they fuelled up the plane, they put all the debris and waste from Union Glacier back onto the plane and the plane flew away and we were shuttled down to our tents. Extremely basic accommodation. I walked into my tent, which was called the Ponting tent—all the accommodation tents were two-man and they were all named after previous Arctic and Antarctic expeditions. So I was in Ponting tent. It was about minus 20, and there was snow on the floor of the tent. It was freezing cold. Beautiful blue sky and the prospect of two 13.1 mile laps around this camp, Union Glacier, with this record dangling at the end of it.

The setup was very austere, though still less austere than the North Pole, which was very much a temporary base, not built for visitors, no mod cons, nothing there. I was quite surprised when we arrived that the base in Antarctica did have toilets—basic toilets, certainly, but permanent ones, and a tiny little shower facility.

It was absolutely freezing, you couldn't contemplate staying very long in those tents. There was snow on the floor, there was absolutely no heating so it's really, really cold. There was one mess tent and you basically did your living in this mess tent because it was heated. The food down there was quite a shock to me, it was almost like a five star restaurant. The volumes that they asked you to eat were certainly incredible. The explanation for that is that you need about 10,000 calories a day to survive in those temperatures just to keep yourself warm, especially if you're going to be active.

Not so easy if you're a vegan. They did try with the vegan food but obviously fresh food down there is a problem. And they tend to emphasise fatty and meat protein-based meals. High calorie porridges, but obviously nothing I could really have, certainly not for breakfast. It was extremely difficult, but I took comfort from the fact that I'd brought a bit of stuff myself and we were only going to be there three days so it would be okay.

So we spent that first night preparing for the race, which we got the okay to run in the next morning. The weather was okay. I remember we arrived in absolutely dazzling bright sun, blue sky—I mean it was just amazing. The glare off the snow down there was incredible. It was indescribably bright. We'd seen the course, it was two laps of 13 miles that they'd plotted out. It all has to be plotted out very strategically because there are craters in the ice. You've got to be so careful where you tread there—even though the ground may look like it's going to be solid it isn't and if you go down one of these glaciers you're going to be out of sight and you're not going to get rescued. They have lost machinery, Ski-Doos and things like that. There's no way of recovering it, there's not machinery to do that.

So we'd seen the course and they kept telling us just head for the Christmas tree on the last lap. And it's like, 'What do you mean the

Christmas tree? There's no trees down here!' But they had a little wooden Christmas tree that they put up out there and you were supposed to head for that and then you'd know when you were nearing camp.

The next morning, Wednesday, it was absolutely freezing. Naturally. I won't say I had a night's sleep, I didn't, I just thought *How am I going to possibly keep warm?* It was so cold. We went to the tent and I slept on and off and then we got up the next morning and we're given the okay to run. Preparing to run one of these races is not just like getting your kit on and lacing your shoes up. It is quite meticulous, your preparation. Everything has to be done absolutely perfectly. Because you can't stop, you can't adjust things on the course, that's not going to happen. You need to set off and be able to keep going, certainly with a view to keep going for 13 miles and then you can come into a warmer place, you can alter and adjust and do what you've got to do and then get back out on the course.

There were two places on the course that you could actually get fluids—and the fluid they were offering was boiled snow. And if you were really, really in problems they had one unmanned tent you could crawl into, and I think there was a radio in there for you to radio back for help. Safety is a big issue down there. They're just setting you off in the Antarctic in the cold; it's a problem. We weren't experienced explorers, and we weren't experienced in these conditions.

So I prepared myself as best I could. I won't say I prepared myself for my run because I didn't think I would be able to run, really, with my knee in the state it was—it was just constantly throbbing and I couldn't bend it past 90 degrees, I really couldn't. But I thought, well, perhaps that's not *too* big an issue because if I've got just *some* movement and I can raise my cadence it's not too bad, because I would never be looking at running at full pace in these conditions anyway. It's not possible to do that when you're running in snow and ice.

I had all these expectations resting on me, guilt, fear, and I honestly didn't know what to do and I didn't know what my plan was going to be. Even putting on the walking boots and grabbing the walking poles, I thought, *If I set off in walking boots, I am destined to be walking 26.2 miles in these conditions.* I didn't even have the kind of cold weather gear you need to walk round in Antarctica. I had running gear. I didn't have the kind of padded gear that you need to be out there for that length of time. It was going to keep me able to run in Antarctica, if I could run, but it wasn't the kind of cold weather gear you needed for walking in those conditions, and I was really scared. The plan I came up with was to see if there was any way I could do something a little bit quicker than a walk on the first lap, and on the second lap come back into the heated tent, put the walking boots on and then just walk that, because if you can walk at say 5K an hour, you're looking at 4–5 hours to do one lap. That's monumental. And truly I just didn't have the equipment for that. That wasn't what I'd come there prepared to do.

But that was the plan, such as it was. We got up on the morning of the race and all you could hear was chitter chatter and excitement and laughing and then the doom and gloom of me, just trudging to the race start.

They called us to the race start and first you have to do all the jolly photo shoots and I really didn't feel like being very jolly at all, I just wanted to get going because it's obviously very cold when you're standing around. I was severely depleted from the Atacama race anyway and I was in a lot of pain, which was terribly worrying. They do say never stand on the start line of a marathon knowing you've got an injury, and now I had a double injury. I had the bad knee, which was now truly bad, and I'm standing on the start line of a marathon—but not just a marathon, a marathon in the middle of Antarctica, after having run six marathons on six continents in an extremely short space of time.

The race set off and everybody just went off like a bullet out of a gun and there were only a few people left around me. I just remember people disappearing into this foggy haze in front of me and I thought *Okay, that's okay. Long day at the office, here we come.* I was just going to run, shuffle, crawl, slide, whatever I had to do. I thought to myself, the job here today is to get the one world record I originally intended to get. Which was to be the quickest woman to complete these marathons between the North Pole and this race. However long this race took me I was just going to have to grin and bear it.

I started at the back of the race, because I thought, *I want everyone out of the way.* I've been kicked in the knee before, when there's a group, at the start of the London Marathon, and certainly when there's a group of exuberant people all trying to keep warm, there's more danger. One guy, he wasn't dressed in a Santa suit, but he had on a Santa hat and a little faux-Santa over-shirt, because it was December, and I remember seeing even him vanish in the fog. And I thought *Oh no, I'm going to get beaten by the man in the Santa suit.* But then I kept reminding myself it wasn't a race, this was something completely different to a race now. It was an endurance test, and it was going to facilitate this world record attempt. I threw out the idea of being the fastest woman in running time because obviously this was going to take me too long, so I was just going to blow off that record attempt. So I set off in Antarctica at what I thought was a half decent tempo. A pace that I was confident was within the realm of my ability, as long as my knee didn't play up too badly.

I don't know where the running came from. I suppose in the moment the adrenaline gets you going and the natural reaction when you are standing under a gantry of a race start is to want to do what comes naturally, which is run. My knee hurt a lot, and I just thought, *Okay, you've got one lap to do and then you can stop. You can stop for as long as you*

155

like. You can put your boots on and you can walk round. That was going to be my treat. But I don't really know how I did it.

As I set off at this steady pace, obviously other people had started off far too quickly, and that's one thing you do not want to do. I'm very good at pace judging. I'm incredibly economical with my pace judging.

So I kept going and kept going and as the kilometers ticked by I realised that I was beginning to catch runners. I caught one guy called Tom who I'd been talking to before the race. And I knew he was a pretty good runner, he was there for the 100K. The marathon was well within his ability, he wasn't stressing and he thought he was running okay and I was going past him. So I thought this perhaps isn't too bad, so long as the knee continues at this pain level and doesn't get any worse, as long as I can just block that out I might be able to just keep going like this.

Obviously you don't check your watch because you can't access it under all the clothing that you're wearing. You wouldn't really waste your time looking anyway, you don't want to take your hands out of your gloves. So I was relying very much on my own judgment of roughly what pace I was running, crawling, whatever I was doing. And I didn't think I was going too badly. I knew I wasn't going to win the race because there were some quite well-established and proficient runners in this race.

So I just chugged on and I remember there was some sort of checkpoint just under 11 miles and I came into it, and I'm a pretty laughy and jokey person, that's the way I cope with things when I'm actually out in trouble, I just laugh about it. I remember in MDS in 2012, being there in this debilitating situation in these appalling conditions and feeling so wretched, and rather than being angry the only thing you can actually do is laugh at yourself. That's what gets me through. So at the 11 mile checkpoint I'm being jolly with the people who are handing out the boiled snow and I said to the race photographer, 'Well that was jolly nice that boiled snow, it really just filled a hole, but I'll just have to move along because I've got a bit of an appointment with 15 more miles of Antarctic terrain.' I told him I was finding this quite difficult. And he said, 'I don't think you're finding it as difficult as a lot of other people are finding it.' That was my first hint.

But I didn't really think too much about it. I set off sort of jogging and up ahead I saw this woman in front of me that I knew was there to win. I couldn't really see too much detail up ahead but I knew there were three runners running in a row, and I knew that the only group of three people was this woman and her two male compatriots who were running with her, to escort her. I thought, *Oh, no. That's her up front. What do I do? Do I just chug on at the pace I'm going ... Or do I just tuck in behind?* Because she'd been billed as being this super triathlete, and I thought *If I do go past her, I'm just going to get into a battle with her because she's obviously going to speed up. I can't catch her because I've got a bad leg.*

So I'm trying to decide if I should hang back, or do I get into this battle of running. Because I am competitive—once I see a chink I am going to try and push. And I didn't want to do something silly and then put myself out of the race altogether. But I weighed it up and I thought, *No, you can't slow down because if you slow down you're going to get hypothermia, you're just going to have to go on, swallow your pride and if she won't let you past you're just going to have to let her go past you, you need to stick at this pace.*

So I decided I would sneak up on the inside and go past—and they realised what I was doing, I heard them talking about it. And after about 800 meters I looked over my shoulder, fully expecting her to be there breathing down my neck—and she was way out in the distance. It was this total epiphany. It was like the Fiona that had been worried and in pain with the knee left my body, and the spirit of a new Fiona came in and it was like, *Wow, perhaps I'm not going that slowly, perhaps this isn't completely out of the window, perhaps I can still salvage something from this race, perhaps I can, dare I think it, break this record of being the fastest woman in actual running time to go to these continents, this bonus world record. And dare I even dream it, that I can win it.*

So that was when the walking boot idea went out of the window and it was whatever this takes, I am going to keep this up. It's going to be either another five hours of trudging, or it's going to be another couple of hours of running if I can maintain this. I decided I was just going to push on and go for the win. I never, ever thought that I could win it in a course record. That did not cross my mind.

But I ran on into the finish at the end of the first lap and I remember just running into the warm tent to grab a new buff and some glasses— because that is the problem, your glasses freeze and your eyes play tricks on you. You see spots and different colored lights. It is tough. So I grabbed that. I didn't feel nutritionally depleted at all because I was running in my comfort zone and I'd only been out there for a couple of hours so that's not too much of a hassle for me.

I'd decided, even though my leg was very, very painful, to stay away from painkillers, because I didn't know how I was going to react to them in those cold conditions. You don't want problems of a stomach nature out there. It's not possible to do anything about it. You're going to be out for a couple of hours and you do not want to need the bathroom. That's not something you want to have to factor in. So I decided that I would just set off, spend as little time as possible in the tent, just grab what I needed and go. I did, and I don't really think I saw another runner up to that point. I don't think there were many others in front of me, I'd caught basically everybody and now it was just a matter of keeping that momentum going to the finish.

But obviously when you're on your second lap you've got the carrot dangling in front of you. You've got the possibility of doing it. It was very, very hard conditions. It was slightly windy, and even a breath of wind out there is going to be cold. But it was also foggy. Not so foggy that you couldn't see a hand in front of your face—because they wouldn't let you run in those conditions—but it was foggy enough that you weren't really aware of where you were running. It was quite eerie. Complete silence. There is nothing. There is no wildlife, just complete silence.

They have these things called sucker holes out there, where the air and everything around you becomes clear all of a sudden. They just appear. One minute you're running in fog and the next minute it's like some curtain's been drawn in front of you and a whole new world just opens up in front around you. It was completely still, motionless, and then it was just like opening a box and looking in. All of a sudden it was beautiful blue sky, just like that, in an instant. So I was running along, trudging along, couldn't see anything, just foggy, snowy conditions, and, all of a sudden, it opened up and you looked around and it was like *Whoa, I am in Antarctica, look at this place. It's absolutely beautiful.* It was majestic. I think that happened at about 15 or 16 miles, the fog just cleared. Bright blue sky and the sun again and it was like running in a completely different place, like you'd just been taken somewhere else. The mountains, the scenery, the ethereal beauty of looking around you and seeing nothing and no one, and, imagine this, I'm in Antarctica. Just feeling it, letting it wash over you. Completely alone in this place that very few people are ever going to be privileged enough to go to, let alone to run a marathon in. It was incredible.

But it's still game on, job to do. I don't really remember too much of the rest of the race, except praying, absolutely praying, that I would be able to continue on. You take nothing for granted in these conditions. You can't. The minute you do you're going to come a cropper. I remember on the last lap of the North Pole Marathon when I'd been running (these were three mile laps), and even with perhaps 800 meters to go to the finish—I could see the camp, I could see the helicopters—even with that short distance to go I wasn't confident that I could complete that race in one piece. You're just so aware of treading this fine line between getting through it and something going wrong. And if it goes wrong you've got no way of making it go right. You just can't. And it hits you very quickly, it really does hit very quickly.

CHAPTER 28

The End of Antarctica

I CONTINUED ON TOWARDS THE finish in Antarctica. I've got little tricks that keep me going. Mum had sewn a lock of my pony's hair into my trousers, so, she said, he'd always be with me. So I was remembering, *Okay, if anything happens, I've got Max with me.* And I had this special little horse necklace that I always wear, that I take great comfort from wearing, knowing it's part of me, part of the sanctuary. I always wear it in races and I'm thinking, I've got that on, I've got this on and my grandad's looking down on me, I'm sure he's looking down on me. And all these things do go through your mind, irrational thoughts. You really are living on the edge out there and those things kept me going.

In the distance I saw a lady runner and I lapped her. She was on her first lap and she was very jolly, she was walking and stopping and just kind of taking it very easy. She was cheering and I looked up and I saw the Christmas tree suddenly. I was nearer than I'd thought, because the previous mile ticker had actually been knocked over, so I'd missed it and I thought I was a mile further down the course than I actually was. So it all came rushing upon me at once, seeing the camp, seeing the gantry, seeing the finish line, and more importantly seeing the tape being held across for the first lady home. And no other runners, nothing, nobody else. And I ran into the finish, broke the tape—nearly broke my neck because I fell over on the tape and slipped.

And it was job done, I'd done it. The cameraman, Dave Painter, came over to me and he just put his arms round me, he said 'You couldn't have done a better job, Fiona, you just couldn't have done any better out there. How you did that I don't know'. And I said, 'Oh, did I win?' That was the only thing, 'Did I win?' And he said, 'Yeah, yeah, you won and you even broke the course record again'. I absolutely couldn't believe that because I knew it was quite a good course record down there and ours hadn't been an ideal run—we had to run the reverse way round on this course, it's slightly quicker if you run the other way around apparently as they'd done in years before, but conditions hadn't permitted that this year. So I couldn't actually believe it.

I ran 4:20.02 and broke the course record, again, and placed up against the men—I came in fourth overall, and my course record's stood for five years. I won that race by about half an hour, and I don't know how I did it.

Honestly I think I was able to do it because I was so desperate to be able to maintain my momentum, not let the animals down, and not let people who help animals down, because they were so supportive of me throughout my running, sending messages. I just didn't want to let anyone down.

I was absolutely elated to win. I'd broken my world records and I've done the job I wanted to do. But with marathons like these you've also got this extra lift that you've actually survived it. I won't say you've beaten Mother Nature or cheated Mother Nature. I always think Mother Nature has allowed you to work with her long enough to get out there and do that. Because when you actually look at it what you're asking of yourself it is a pretty big ask. You're asking to go out there and do something that is already physically demanding in easy conditions, in easy terrain and a nice climate, traversing 26.2 miles. And you're asking yourself to do it in these conditions in this place that is basically the bottom of the Earth. You're blessed to be there in the first place, let alone running marathons there. So you don't feel you've cheated Mother Nature, you feel honoured that she's allowed it to happen, allowed you to be strong enough to actually go out and do it.

My knee did hurt, but I have to say that I think a lot of the pain I was suffering in my knee was also worry and stress, because it wasn't just a knee that hurt, it was a knee that hurt and I had to get my gear on and run a marathon with this knee that hurts, so each time I bent it before the race, every movement I made, the pain was accentuated by the anticipation and stress of what was ahead.

And of course you get back and there isn't some great congratulatory celebration, because there are so few people there. The course is not lined with spectators or anything like that. There are crew down there for the actual Union Glacier base, there are other expeditions going on, people preparing to go out like Richard Parks was. Other cameramen filming documentaries or whatever, but there isn't a great entourage of people there to celebrate. So your celebrating is very much done on your own, internally.

I wouldn't say the pain went away, because it didn't, it was bad all the time I was down there, but it subdued a little bit. After the race, they'd promised us all a hot shower. They'd got a temporary short stay shower block where you could go in for a minute—one minute—and have a shower. They prepared that there for the runners since after the race you're totally depleted of energy and you need to warm up. And obviously you've run a marathon so they figured we'd like to be clean.

But after the race that wasn't particularly tantalizing to me. It was a pretty inhospitable thought, going back to the freezing Ponting tent. So I got changed and got out on the course to stand for as long as I could near the finish line and greet the runners that were going to finish later than me. It was really nice to share in their celebration, help make the moment special for them. That was wonderful.

I did have a satellite phone, and I knew my mum had been worried, when I'd been going off on this challenge. And I worry too. One of my priorities when I'm away from the sanctuary is to make sure that I've got some contact so I know what's going on. We didn't know about sat phones when I went to the North Pole and somebody there suggested it after the incidents that had happened at the North Pole. We were without a sat phone up there and the group could have done with one. So my mum came up with the money to buy one—she used the money she'd saved up for her funeral. She decided she wasn't going to have a funeral. Not that she's planning to die, but she gave me that money to get a sat phone so at least I could be in contact when I was away. It's is very detrimental to me psychologically to feel that I'm absolutely out of contact, that I can't be asked any questions or that there might be things at the sanctuary that I know that probably Martin doesn't know. I like to check in on the animals.

So I rang Martin on the sat phone and told him, and I rang my mum, who was back in Punta Arenas, and it was just like euphoria. Martin started to line up the media contacts that I'd made. A guy from the *Daily Mirror*, he wanted to do a story, and there was lots and lots of interest.

When I got back to the tent, the tricky part was that the weather started to close in at that point. It was extremely dubious as to whether the 100K would be able to go ahead. The marathon was on the Wednesday, the 100K was going to be on the Friday and we were going to leave on the Saturday.

But with the weather being what it was, they didn't know that the 100K was going to be able to go ahead. Bearing in mind that there are only a few entries for running a 100K in Antarctica, and they're probably going to take a while. They need to allow 24 hours out there in those conditions. Yes, a quick runner isn't going to take 24 hours to run 100K, but some of the slower runners need more time obviously. And you don't want to pay a lot of money to go to Antarctica to enter a 100K and then find that you've only done 85K and you're lifted out and you don't get to finish it.

But by the morning of the 100K, after we'd spent Thursday just recovering, playing jigsaws and doing whatever you do in Antarctica in a small tent when you're absolutely stuck there, one of the other runners, Tom, who had done the marathon but only really gone to run the 100K, had become ill. Tom said, 'I don't think I'm well enough to run the 100K'. He was really, really disappointed because he is an ultrarunner, he's not a marathon runner really. So he looked for volunteers who would go round each lap with him, and stay with him and help him as much as they could. And the 100K had no interest to me in Antarctica, but Tom and his partner Cat had been really friendly to me, and Tom was terribly poorly. So when he asked for volunteers to go round with him, do one lap with him, I volunteered.

The 100K was ten laps of 10K, and you can't give somebody a piggy back, that's ridiculous, but being out there and being alone, I have to emphasise, is very frightening and things come upon you so quickly that you do get scared. Because, yes, okay, the Ski-Doos might find you collapsed in the ice and then you might not die, but you could do real permanent damage to your health if you get problems out there. And 10K is not far on the road, it's not far on a trail, but it is a long way out there, alone in the snow, cold, knowing you've got nine laps or eight laps or seven more of these laps to do. It is a daunting experience, psychologically and physically.

So I said, 'Okay, I'll do it, I don't mind'. He and Cat had been good to me, they'd taken me under their wing, I was sitting with them and I didn't feel so alone. I faced a lot of hostility from certain people in that camp, and it wasn't a good time. I don't know what I'd have done without Tom and Cat, just completely being ignored in this tent. They were really embracing of my veganism—Cat was a vegetarian and she was also fire crew, so we had a fair amount in common. And if it's not going to be any great hassle to help anyone—even if it is—I felt it would always be in my heart to go and do it. My dream had been fulfilled as far as I was concerned, and I wanted them to fulfill theirs. I wanted to help Tom. Cat couldn't run with him, she wasn't up to it, she just said, 'I can't do it'.

So I said, 'Well I don't mind doing it'. After all, how many chances are you going to have to go running in Antarctica? It's an opportunity just to be out there. So I went round the 100K with him. And oh, we went through some monumental battles out there. Poor Tom really wasn't very well. He'd got a flu or something. And being poorly in Antarctica is not good, having to go back to these freezing tents. He really did suffer. But we got through it, we played all sorts of games, I made him remember all the names of my horses, my dogs. We chatted, we talked, we laughed, we cried, and each lap, my job was that when we got to about 9K or so I would run on ahead and tell Cat what he needed. He'd tell me, 'I need some soup' 'I need this, I need that, I need a new buff' or whatever. So

I'd run on ahead and tell her and she'd be there waiting for him when he came in.

Because obviously these laps were taking a long time. People think 10K, what's that, like under 40 minutes? No, no, it can be like two and a half hours if you're walking like we were. That's when I realised that my gear, the gear that I'd run in at the North Pole, the gear that I'd run in here in Antarctica and that I thought was the 'best stuff' you could possibly have for running—it probably is. But it's not the best stuff for walking, it's not that warm. And I was getting cold myself because I hadn't gotten the gear to be out there trekking.

Somehow we held it together. I remember at one point having to literally go behind him and push him through the snow. It was difficult, but it was really, really good at the end. Coming up to the last lap, the sun began to come out. It had been terribly foggy when we started, but about 20 hours later when we finished this monumental, epic experience, the sun came out, and being able to pull off the course and let him finish, on his own—it was amazing, how it perked him up, just seeing the finish line.

That was a big plus, actually, being able to help somebody else out there. That's always a big plus. I like there to be a reason behind me being out there, always. But after that race, Tom basically took to his bed. He was very poorly the rest of the time we were there.

As I said, it was our intention to fly out on a Saturday, but, unfortunately, the weather closed in. And when the weather closes in in Antarctica, it's just no go. The whole camp went into lockdown. It was cordoned off, and you were not allowed to do anything. The blizzards, the snow, and the cold were incredible. It really was like one of those *Scott of the Antarctic* scenes that you imagine.

Richard Parks, who was supposed to be going off on this solo expedition to the South Pole, he was grounded. He was waiting for days.

You couldn't do a thing. You couldn't even see a hand in front of your face.

So we were all confined in this tiny warm tent. You were really disorientated. You didn't know whether it was day or night. And you found yourself doing bizarre things—like, who snacks on peanuts at one in the morning? You didn't even realise it was one in the morning. One guy I kept calling the Cookie Monster, because he was unable to control himself with the biscuits. It was like 'What are you doing? You're back on the biscuits'. He was a doctor. He said, 'I'm going to leave here so huge'. Because that's the thing, there was always a massive supply of food that they baked, cream cakes and all that. They always had food there for the people that are constantly coming in to maintain the base. So I think a lot of the guys that could eat that food were spending all their time eating. I couldn't eat it, so I didn't have much to eat at all. And that pretty much lasted until the end of the following week.

Then there were some tense bits, because we did get a few opportunities where it looked like we could fly out of Antarctica. The weather was beautiful where we were, and the frustration became apparent, because a lot of the people who do these races are quite wealthy. It's probably 10,000, 12,000 euros to enter, so you've got to have money to enter them. I remember there were some businessmen from Azerbaijan who were *desperate* to get back to their construction company, and they simply did not understand that no matter how much money you've got, no matter what strings you can pull and who you know, you ain't leaving, because nobody will come. It's not safe. They couldn't get it into their heads that it was beautiful, beautiful weather in Antarctica, but, unfortunately, the weather in Punta Arenas wasn't good enough to launch this plane supplied for this mission. There are only a couple of planes that they dare send into Antarctica, these big workhorse kind of Russian planes, Aleutians.

Our plane looked like it had a very angry face at the front with teeth in it. It was a real monumental beast, this thing that they take out there. It's not a commercial airline plane, it's actually a haulage plane that they use to take all the supplies into Antarctica in.

Apparently you have to be an incredibly experienced pilot to fly into Antarctica, because it's surrounded by mountains and you've got this tiny little airstrip to land on, which is ice, so you've got to know what you're doing. This Russian pilot was very proud to tell me he'd done a hundred missions there. It is frightening. It's really, really frightening when you're taking off in this plane and landing. Everything's rocking and you've got popping going on from oil drums, and everything's rolling around.

We were stranded down there for ten days. Food was getting short. Tempers were getting short, also. People were getting angry. People were desperate to get out of there, but, as I say, if you can't take off and you can't land, they won't come.

I had my sat phone, and they were begging me to ring back to Punta Arenas and find out exactly what was going on there. My mum kept having to leave the hotel she was based in and go up to the airstrip and see if this plane could take off. And it just couldn't. Couldn't come. So we were stuck in Antarctica for another week after the race.

The plane eventually did come for us. We all piled on and we went back to Punta Arenas. Then I only got a few hours in Punta Arenas to recover myself and get to the airport to fly home, because unfortunately, the pressure was on for me to go home to care for the sanctuary and the animals there. Martin had been at the sanctuary all this time that I'd been in the Atacama Desert and Antarctica, and stranded in Antarctica. He'd used all his holiday days up and his work was saying he had to come in to work or his job would be in jeopardy.

So we turned around, got an emergency flight back to Santiago and then on to Paris and finally London. We got back in the early hours of Sunday. When we were in Punta Arenas and I got back to see my mum, who had been stranded in this hotel with *nothing*, I felt so sorry for her. I think it was worse being stranded there than it was in Antarctica. Even the hotel had become too full. They hadn't got a room for my mum because they thought we were going to be leaving a week earlier. They found her some sort of cupboard to stay in because they felt so sorry for her. I fully expected to walk in and find scratches on the wall of the days that she'd been left there. She hadn't got any money and her credit card wouldn't work. She couldn't get them to understand, at the desk. It was all quite complicated.

But even with all these setbacks and complications, during all it I was thinking *This is fantastic. I've spoken to Martin. We've got all this media and press that are interested. Crikey, they were so interested after the North Pole Marathon that they invited me to the BBC, what are they going to do after I've done this?* We were really excited. And my mum said, 'Well, if Martin's work is in jeopardy and at risk, you're going to have to do national. No local news, you can't waste your time with that, it's got to be national'.

How little did we know.

CHAPTER 29

The Holidays

WE FLEW HOME FROM ANTARCTICA quite on a high. Then we got home and it was like getting stuck with pins, deflating more and more. December was a low. Nobody was interested in the story. I mean we rang all the people that said they'd be interested in this harebrained idea—'We're very interested, come back when you've done it'. We rang the journalist at the *Daily Mirror* that said he would be really keen to do an article on this amazing achievement from this British woman. When we got back initially, we couldn't get him to say why, he just said, 'We haven't got room'. He actually said, 'Have you tried local?' I said, 'Well, it's not local is it? What, local Antarctic news? It's got no relevance locally. It's international almost, I've been to every continent'. And in the end, he explained. It's not always down to the journalists, what they can put in their newspapers, magazines, and on their programs. He said, 'It's December, it's coming up to Christmas, the emphasis is very much on advertising food. Food at

Christmas is meat, dairy, extravagant products, animal derivative products and the advertisers are what pays the wages. We're not going to upset them by one minute advertising a five bird roast and the next minute running a story saying 'you don't need it, look what this amazing vegan woman has done". He said, 'It's just not possible for me to do it'.

I was so disappointed. I was absolutely gutted, to be truthful. It nearly broke me. It really did nearly break me. And we had it from several sources. I thought, what is the point? Why have I done all this? I was absolutely distraught. Not for myself, but for the reason I'd done it. I had put an enormous amount of effort into it. The logistics of it all, and the little things that people don't even consider.

It's not just about the distances. It's about the different terrains and the logistics of being on different continents to run these distances in such a short space of time. For instance, I was running at 14,400 feet in the Atacama Desert, up the side of a volcano. Incredibly hot. No oxygen. Completely different conditions to what I would expect myself to do it in five days later, having flown down to Antarctica, another continent, and run a marathon in minus 20 in snow and ice. Just a completely different set of circumstances that I've got to be adjusted to within an extremely short space of time. Added to that, I went around (I wouldn't say I ran) 100K with a fellow competitor, two days later, in Antarctica, purely because I'd got the energy and I'd got the ability to do so. I'd got the ability within me to help him achieve his goal, which was to do that 100K. I'd done all that within seven days or eight days. It's a big ask, but it's what I consider myself blessed to be able to do.

In that period when you're trying to do these records you're living under complete and utter pressure. When you've done a race, you don't feel any relief that you've done that one. You're just panicking. Will I be able to do the next one? Will everything hold together for the next one?

The logistics of even trying to pack bags that you can keep with you at all times, with your essential running gear. When you are going to do a race in really hot, high altitude conditions, but you also need to keep with you all the stuff that you need to run in the Antarctic five days later. Even the amount of flying causes stress—air conditioning on planes, are you going to pick up a bug, are you going to pick up a virus? You can't run with those things, so you want to live in a bubble, and it does create a very stressful situation for yourself and for those around you. Which you then feel guilty about, because you are constantly saying, 'Have you got a cold? Because I don't want you near me if you have. You've got to go into your room'. It's really difficult. And I felt guilty that I put my loved ones through all that for no apparent reason.

What came next was a lot of collecting myself. I'm not going to lie and say, 'But I bounced back and was all brave and "You're not going to beat me"'. It didn't happen like that. I was so upset by it. It felt like confirmation of the suspicion I had that whatever I did wouldn't work out. I mean, surely there should be more interest in this feat. This was actually quite good. Even by my standards, and I don't think everything I do is good by virtue of the fact that I do it. I will try to look objectively and assess what I've done. And even when I don't particularly like something, I can appreciate it for what it is. I have that ability. I knew along the way that I was being overlooked. But I just thought, y'know, the face doesn't fit. Okay, the face doesn't fit.

It did take me a while to pick myself up. Especially in December, when there is so much emphasis on meat and dairy products, and the celebrating, the so called season of celebration, which so many people choose to celebrate with death. I always find December difficult in that way. Obviously, it should be a time for family, it should be a time for joy. But it seems to be that to celebrate that, people think they have to have these animal products, which is just so wrong to me, I can't even begin to explain. It's difficult to get my head around.

I was down through December. I was down going into January because I was facing another year during which I was going to feel compelled to battle for the animals but not actually know if it's worth doing it. And when I say worth doing it, of course, every life is worth it. *Every* life is worth it. But tangibly, here I've got these physical lives at the sanctuary I can battle for and I can raise funds for; I can get some more grazing land so I can take some more cattle. I've got these voiceless animals I desperately want to encourage others not to abuse, not to exploit. So the question is, is running worth my time at this point? For every race I run I've got to invest a lot of time, and effort, and energy, and mental discipline, and strength. Should I just spend all that time and effort and energy on the sanctuary, on the animals I care for?

CHAPTER 30

Marathon des Sables Redux

THAT WAS WHEN I THOUGHT, *Well, what am I going to do next? I'll either just forget it all, or, I've got these world records, what's the next thing?*

Coming up in April I had a place in the 2014 Marathon des Sables. The question was whether I wanted to continue. I had the endurance for it, the last year had shown that. Seven marathons on seven continents, plus the North Pole, and after some time recovering I wasn't any worse for it, physically.

I think in the end it was that underlying drive I've always had that decided things. I hadn't done what I wanted to in MDS in 2012, I hadn't accomplished what I'd set out to, and I had the chance now to make a better job of it. I felt the need to take that opportunity—and ideally not go out there with broken toes.

And too, I think perhaps in a way the pressure was off a bit. After the enormous stress of the world record attempt, and the sheer physical demands of accomplishing what I'd accomplished in the last months, one race that would be over in seven days didn't seem as bad as all that. Perhaps it was foolish of me to think that way, but when you've been in that state of stress I'd been in for so long something's got to give. And possibly for me that something was my ability to maintain that emotional state. I won't say I was cavalier about it, but it didn't feel like much more than something I needed to get out there and check off. I did the training and packed my bag and went off to Morocco. I didn't join any of the forums and the groups and invest heavily in that sort of chit-chat and race nitter-natter before I went out there. I didn't know anybody else that was in the race. I just thought, *I'm going to go out there and do my thing, and that will be that.*

The format had changed slightly from when I'd done it before. In 2012, you went out the day before, on Thursday. You stayed in a hotel. You were able to form a few bonds with people. You had to share a room with someone. I'd shared a room at a hotel with a guy and a girl and we decided we were going to stay together in the race, and then we met some more people who looked like rather unlikely candidates to be running this race and we kind of all gelled together. We developed a bond before we arrived in the desert at the camp. This time they just flew you directly into the desert to a very small airport and then trucked you out to where the race was going to be held. So you'd only had a chance to meet and converse with people on the plane or on the bus going out to the race start. The seat next to me on the plane was empty, and then the guy I'd sat next to on the bus going out to the race was a bit of a gibbering wreck, because he was coming back from the year before when he hadn't completed it and he was terribly nervous.

So that's eight hours into the desert on coaches, to where the race camp is. The camp is just a big circular line of the open-sided tents. The international runners—international to me, obviously I'm international to them, but what I call non-Brits and non-English speakers tend to be in the middle part and on the outer ring is English speakers, Americans and people like that.

We arrived at camp after dark. I didn't know anyone. I had learned from my experience in 2012 that the camp is always set up the same, and the tent you get in and its proximity to the finish line will be the same every night. So I clocked that it was better to get in a tent that was going to be near to the finish, because when you do finish, you are completely spent. They hand you about six litres of water, which you've got to carry back to your tent. You don't really feel like walking very far at that point.

So I went down the line and I'm calling into these tents, 'Any room in here?' No. 'Any room in here?' No. I got to this tent that looked practically empty apart from one guy standing there, a nice-looking, friendly guy. I said, 'Any room in this tent?' He explained that one half of the tent was taken with him and his mates, who would be along later, but the other half was completely free. I like to go in the corner of the tent so I can keep myself to myself. It's also slightly better if you get any more men in the tent because they're bigger and they need more head room and I don't need a lot of head room. So I decided that that was going to be my little place for the week or nine days that we're out there. There wasn't anything to do at that point, so I just sat there waiting for his friends to come along, and anybody else who wanted to settle in our tent. After a bit his three chums came back to the tent, and they were all great big strapping guys, six footers plus.

The people who were still searching for a tent space, they're walking around with head torches, shining them in. 'Any room in this tent?' It's pitch black, it's the desert. It's getting cold. One more senior lady came along, Moira, a very nice lady. Then a lovely girl called Vicky, who looked kind of nervous. I invited her in and she introduced herself, said she was a barrister.

Then Mike came along, very much later. Mike Julian had a painful story behind his race in the desert. He explained to us that he had leukemia and he was on chemotherapy. It was touch and go as to whether he would be allowed to run. He'd come with all sorts of doctors' and solicitors' letters and goodness knows what as well, for liability, taking away the organisers' responsibility of allowing him to run the race. Saying that he was fit to run. Saying that he could probably get through it. Even when we did the race checks the following day it was still uncertain they were going to allow him to even start. They agreed in the end though.

The next morning you get up and you have to go and have everything weighed, all your medical certificates checked to make sure they're all endorsed properly. They check that you've got all the equipment, the mandatory equipment they require you to have. They give you various life-saving things like flares that they want you to carry, salt tablets; they drill in the fact that you've got to take what they give you. You've got to keep it with you. You could be stopped at any point during the race and be asked to produce it so you can't just get rid of this stuff. It's very heavy. You go through all that and then you hand in your civvy bag and then you're just left stripped in what you're going to wear for the race. What's in your backpack for the race and your clothing, that's all you've got for the following week. So it's hello desert, goodbye civilization, this is going to be difficult.

I hadn't acclimatised, because you arrive and you've got literally one day to experience the heat, the camp, all this change of circumstance before the start of the race. We settled down, and I wasn't actually too stressed out by it all because I'd been through the procedure before. I'd almost got a little bit of a gung ho attitude about the whole thing.

Thinking, *I'm just here. I'm probably going to try and enjoy this as much as I possibly can. It's time to be alone. I'm very privileged to be in the desert. I've got experience. I know what I'm doing, I've got a rough idea now. Let's just hit it and see how it goes.*

I think it's better to err on the side of caution at the start of the week. Always, the plan is, if you have the energy in the long stage, that is where you will hit it. Because you can lose much more time in the long stage than you can ever gain in the shorter stages. Because I'm not a mega experienced desert runner. It's not something that I do all the time. It's a completely different technique, as different as 100 meter running is to marathon running. It's still running, but it's very different running. But we set off on the first day and I was confident in my pack and everything that I had and I knew where I wanted to be. I knew what my plan was.

At the end of the first day I was first back to the tent by a long way, miles in front of everyone. When you arrive back to your tent, which the Berbers have set up for you, there's basic cover and that's as far as it goes. If you are camping on stony ground, there will be stones underneath the carpet. It will literally be like lying on a bed of stones. Likewise if there are prickly bushes. It's not that comfortable. They don't clear everything for you. If you want it cleared that's your responsibility.

So I got back to the tent, not particularly fatigued by the day's activities, even though it really was a heck of a stage. I think there were 15 miles of sand dunes. And the first day, when your packs are heaviest, we had to run across a short dried-up salt lake and hit dunes. We hit dunes so bad and so hard that I can't even explain. It was a kind of baptism of fire. But I arrived at the tent feeling not too bad. Got changed. You need something to change into so I take this tiny little vest top. Thought, right, I'll clear the tent now and I'll make sure the area's all nice. Because a lot of people think that as a vegan, you're just going to sit in your ivory tower, you're going to moan and groan at everything, you're going to be antisocial. I wanted to make it clear that wasn't the case. You can't literally hoover and put the kettle on and make a coffee but you can make it as pleasant as you can for people when they do arrive back.

Moira came back to the tent after about ten hours. And I was so relieved to see her, because I had looked at her and thought, *You might be an extremely tough lady, but this is a tough race. I really hope you're okay out there.* So I was relieved to see her. I thought, *Thank heaven for that. She's got through the first day.* I went over and I congratulated her. She said, 'I never got out of the first set of sand dunes. I've come back in a car. I've packed'. She was absolutely gutted by the experience. I was still writing to her long after it. I don't know if she really ever recovered from pulling out of the race.

The next day, at one point my nose started to bleed and one of the other guys in the race said, 'Do not let the race organisers see your nose bleeding'. I asked, 'Why not?' He said, 'Because they'll think you've got Ebola'. It was just when Ebola broke out. He said, 'They're paranoid about Ebola right now. So if your nose is bleeding, that's one sign. Don't let them see your nose bleed'. So I was attempting to cover that up as well.

I think I was in about eighth place on the second day. Notwithstanding the nosebleed, I was doing well. It was coming easily to me. I wasn't forcing the issue. I was going my pace and doing my thing. I arrived back at the tent first. I'd settled down, it was getting dark, and Mike came back to the tent.

He looked dreadful. He looked like he'd been through a war zone. He probably had, in his own way. Not a physical fighting war zone, but he was obviously battle-scarred. He came back into the tent and he said, 'I'm packing. I can't do it'. I said, 'Look, Mike, you might feel better in the morning. You might feel better'.

I had my fuel burner on and I was making myself a drink. I remember that I was able to use what I'd gotten, my Esbit tablets, to heat this drink I'd made and I gave him the drink and I said, 'Look, let's just talk about it before you go and do it', because once you go over into what they call the white zone, where the race organisers are, which is slightly more plush and not so austere—once you go over there, you're out of the race. We were in the black zone.

I said, 'Let's just talk about it'. He said, 'Look, even if I could get through tomorrow I'm not going to do the long stage, I can't do it, I can't remember my chemo, I'm just not able to do it'. I think he was understandably frightened of being out there alone with his condition. Over the course of the long stage—the distance of which varies every year but is generally somewhere in the realm of 80K—you're going to be more alone than usual because the distance and the spread of runners is going to be so much greater than in a shorter distance like a marathon where the runners are going to be more bunched. It's done at night and people are frightened of being out in the desert alone at night, navigating their own way when you can't see anyone else. People have got lost in this race. There's a story of a Russian guy who got lost for something like nine days, and the drink your own urine situation comes up. Let's just say the prospect of that stage isn't soothing.

With all that in mind, I said to Mike, 'How about this. Focus on tomorrow, decide tomorrow's the end of your race and get through it, and then if you decide you want to tackle the long stage then it becomes our race and I will stay with you'. And at first he told me I couldn't do that because I was doing so well, and I said 'C'mon, what am I doing well for? I want to complete, but I want you to complete. I've done it once, I've got one medal. I want you to get yours'. And I think when people hear this they think I'm crazy, to give up a better place in the race in order to help someone maybe complete. Well, am I crazy? Because we think we're compassionate as a people, we think as humans our natural reaction should be to help someone in need. If you needed help you would hope that somebody would help you. There's no doubt about that. So why would you then not want to help someone if they needed help and you can offer that kindness? I don't understand that.

So we left it at that, and we set off the next day and I did my thing again and I added another good stage. I felt really prepared for the long stage the next day. I'd saved a lot of the stuff I had brought with me so I knew I had plenty of nutrition for the long day. I'd taken a few gels, which I never usually use but there are some that I can just about cope with and you have to take a couple because you can't carry great quantities of nutrition, and these things slip in quite nicely.

I thought the long stage was looking positive. I had an end goal time in mind and I stuck to that. Mike didn't come back to camp and I went to bed thinking *I hope to God he's all right.* I thought perhaps he'd made the decision out there to pull. I didn't really know what to think, if I'm going to be a hundred percent truthful and honest. In a way I suppose from where I was and the way I was feeling there was some hope he had pulled out, because then I could at least run my race. I would be a liar to say that it didn't cross my mind and I don't want to lie.

But then I heard clapping around the race finish and I went over to look and it was Mike. He'd come back and the first thing he did when he walked into camp was put his arms around me and say, 'Does the offer stand for tomorrow, because I want to do the long stage', and what do you say? 'No, I was only kidding, go away'. Of course you don't, c'mon. I told him yes, of course it stood. We went back to the tent and we sat there and discussed it, talked about what the plan would be. This other woman, Vicky, who is the epitome of a strong, together woman, a criminal barrister specializing in sexual abuse, she said 'Well actually, if you're going to walk round with Mike, is there any chance that I can come with you too? Because I just don't think I'm up to it either'. So I said okay, this is the plan and we stick to this plan. This is the way we hit this race. And they were brilliant.

We had a hard time out there. It's not easy in the desert in the middle of the night when you're alone and you're tired, and my problem was I was out there longer than I wanted to be out there, than I'm used to being out, because I'm used to basically finishing quite quickly and then getting off my feet and I don't like stopping for too long. But to be fair, we weren't stopping, we were trying to rush through the checkpoints. Not sit down, just grab what we needed and go. But it was just taking an awful long time. I was thinking *Oh my lord. If I was to run ten miles on the road, it would take me under an hour. At this rate it's going to take me four hours.*

We did have a heck of a time. Mike was very poorly. I mean, you can't be out there in these conditions putting yourself through that on chemotherapy without struggling. I take my hat off to him. He really did lay it out to finish that stage and I think part of what kept him going was that he wasn't just doing it for himself. He was doing it for the community of people whose eyes were on him, who were in a similar position, thinking that their life had ended because they'd got a similar condition. It was prohibitive, they thought they'd never do the things that they'd loved to do before this condition afflicted them, and he wanted to prove you could. You could get over, you could kick its arse, you could do anything. So, there were a lot of people out there relying on him to do this and not fail, and he knew that.

It was an extremely long day at the office. We got in to the finish. We just about hit the goal. I said we don't really want to be out there and see the sun rising the next morning because that's when it gets hot again and we don't want two lots of that. We did get back to camp. The mood was obviously great then.

The next day came along, and with it the last marathon stage, which I was first home in, purely because I just wasn't tired. Most people are clapped out after the long stage but I wasn't, because I'd been out there a long time yes, but I was out drudging about, not pushing myself harder than I ever have. I'm used to drudging about at the sanctuary, I'm on my feet a long time—they're long, hard physical days. So the long stage hadn't taken that much out of me, it certainly hadn't taken what I had hoped doing that long stage would take out of me, when I was thinking I was going to be pushing myself to my utmost. So, I toddled off and I did my bit in the marathon stage, the last official race stage, and I was very pleased with that. The next day was a charity stage and it wasn't a competitive stage of the race. I felt really good, buoyant.

People questioned why I'd done what I did for Mike. It wasn't easy to explain to them at the time, because there's not a great deal of opportunity to explain when you're out there in the desert. It genuinely was about practicing compassion. I would do it again. I mean, competition's fine but compassion is worth a lot more. I don't regret doing what I did. Yes, it's left me with the question of what might've been, but after all I might've gone flying off in the long stage and broke my leg, as runners have done in the past. Even race leaders have come into the finish line and fallen and broken a femur. What is, is, and I can't change that.

It's a good learning experience. It's not just about running a race. I think it's also a graphic illustration of how little you can survive on. The ingenuity you have to use to be able to survive, and be able to do this incredibly arduous task, and how much we waste in a normal day-to-day situation. This prodigious waste of both food and resources.

If you go into that race and you embrace it for what it is, it's not just a stinking seven days in the Sahara Desert and brownie points, 'I've done that and I've got a medal'. If you take away and adapt parts of it into your normal daily life, and others did the same, it would be a better world.

For instance, even now every time I turn the tap on and can take a drink, I appreciate that drink, even though it's only tap water. If you haven't got anything to drink I can't tell you how beautiful tap water tastes. The same with food. The same with rest. Just not having to get up and do it again, or not having this discomfort of sand everywhere, and not having a moment's peace, you really appreciate the things you have got, rather than always aspiring to have things that you don't need. Things you don't actually want, you just want them because they're there. It gives you the ability to appreciate things in a different a dimension. The little things that a lot of people take for granted, I don't take for granted now. Not that I ever really have, but I certainly don't since I've done MDS.

So, I knew I was capable of doing that kind of ultrarunning, but when I had finished, I didn't really know what to do next. It was all becoming very real to me then that doing all these things is fine but getting publicity for doing them is very difficult. So I came back home and by then it was the end of April, and I thought *What do I do next? Do I do anything at all, or do I knock the running on the head?* I didn't really know. But strangely enough about a month later BBC Radio London contacted me and I was invited on a sports show. They said 'We would like you to come on to chat about this amazing running that you do, somebody's told us about it and we think it's really incredible, the variety of what you do is amazing'.

Bearing in mind this is a sport show. This isn't somebody who doesn't understand about running, who just thinks 'Wow that sounds amazing', this is somebody who does understand about running and says 'Wow, I think that's amazing'. So, I went off to London and I remember that the guy on before me on that radio show was a very high-profile footballer. I think it was Wayne Rooney. So this was a pretty high-profile show. And I went on there for ten minutes to talk about running.

So I start talking about my running, and the interviewer and the producer were very receptive towards me, which is quite unusual because as I've said to people, you can really only be as good or as bad as the interviewer allows you to be. Interviewing people is a profession, it's a skill. It's what they do and they know how to lead a conversation to get the best or worst out of a subject.

So they're asking about my running and I told them 'Yes, I've run the North Pole, I've run MDS, I've run 2:38 in a road marathon. I've got top 20s in London, Berlin, Amsterdam,' and it was going really positively. It came up to the newsbreak and the interviewer said 'Look, I've been looking you up on the internet, doing a bit more research. I just thought you were a runner, I didn't realise there's all these other things as well—you've got an animal sanctuary'.

'Yep, I've got an animal sanctuary', I said, and he said 'you know there's something else strange about you' and I thought, *What, like fire brigade?* And he said 'You're a vegan'. I said 'yes, I'm a vegan'. He said, 'you can touch on that if you want'. So when we returned from the break I talked about the sanctuary, and he thought it was amazing that I could fit all this in. He actually said when are you going to write a book, when is there going to be a film about you, because this is so amazing the way you're churning all this different stuff out. Then he said 'There's something else isn't there?' and I said 'Yes—I'm vegan, and I have been all my adult life and most of my childhood and I'm proud of that'.

My intent was to show all the sports people that it's possible. I wanted to serve as an example. I don't want to shout down people's throats, I don't want to rub it in their faces, but if you are considering this lifestyle and if the thing that's making you reluctant to try it is that perhaps you will not be able to perform athletically at a high standard, then perhaps you can look at what I've done and say she's done it, so we do have an example, we've got proof. It can be done. It's like when I was back in the Halstead Marathon. The town councilwoman said to my mum, 'I've seen it with my own eyes'. I've heard that so many times. I heard it in Omsk. 'Thank you for coming here and letting my parents see you doing this with their own eyes'. Because you can be told, you can be shouted at, but you as a vegan athlete are a tangible thing. You're there and you're doing it and you've done it for a long time, and they don't see a weak person, they don't see anyone who's a social misfit. They just see a normal person who happens to be plant based and very passionate about that doing extreme things.

I was on the radio show for about twenty-five minutes, and after that show I got so much positivity on the internet and in the media. The response was like Wow, you do all that on your own? You unload lorries, you don't find it difficult to go and stack four thousand bails of hay? You're on the fire brigade? You run these marathons, you've been to the North Pole, where does it end?

It ends where it starts. At veganism; at this is what I can do, whether it's mentally or physically. I'm at one with myself. When people ask me if I think I could have done any better, could have been a better runner, on another diet, my answer is no, I couldn't have been a better runner on any other diet, because this is me. This is me and anybody who knows sport knows that when you stand on a start line, you need to be mentally ready. That's why sports psychology is a science, and I know psychologically I don't want to feel that I'm here at the cost and expense of someone suffering elsewhere. I'm here, I'll do the suffering. I do the suffering with my own leg, I know what suffering is and I really don't want to be a part of anybody else having that inflicted on them.

CHAPTER 31

The Rio Marathon

IN JULY 2014 I DECIDED TO run the Rio Marathon in South America. The only problem was, I'd decided to enter at the last minute, literally a week before the race. I'd come back from MDS in April and though there was a nice wave of positivity and publicity attached to that and that radio show I did, there was also a great deal of negativity coming my way as well. It got to the point where I was seriously considering again whether or not I should pack it all in with the running. To combat that idea, and to sort of fight negativity with positivity, I decided to run the South American leg of my world record again, and go for a shorter time—try to break my own record with a race I could run faster than the Volcano Marathon I'd run in the Atacama Desert. But by the time I had that idea straight in my mind, the Rio Marathon was one week away, and after the Rio one the South American marathons kind of dried up. There aren't that many in South America, even now.

So we started the process of trying to get a place in the Rio Marathon, but we'd missed the entries period. The online entries were closed and we couldn't get an answer from the race as to whether I could enter. There was an English site but they weren't answering queries from it. The Rio Marathon is the biggest race in South America, quite a high profile race. Finally I thought *Well, I've written for a place, and it's too late to get an elite start, obviously they don't want me in the race, I'm not good enough.* But then they did get back to me and they said yes, it would be wonderful to have you come over, we'd love to have you running. So I literally decided a couple of days before the race that I'd do this Rio Marathon in an attempt to get a quicker marathon time. Just to address the negativity in my life, really. I wanted to prove over again that I could get some good out of this running thing.

So I toddled off to this massive marathon. I hadn't quite expected how big it would be. It was a very big race. We were incredibly lucky actually that when we booked our hotel I'd insisted that when we arrived at the airport we get somebody to transfer us to the hotel, because I wasn't relying on myself to get cabs and find where I was going in a short space of time, when I was piling off this long haul flight, piling into a hotel and then piling off to a race. I just didn't know how I could do it, especially with the language barrier.

So we asked the travel company to book us a taxi from the airport to where we were staying in Rio, and fortunately, the taxi driver was lovely, bless him. His name was Yuri, and he was a fluent English speaker. He told us if we had any problems while we were there, to contact him and he would help us.

Little did I know, but the whole thing actually pivoted on Yuri. Because even though this is a big international race with a lot of runners from abroad, the language barrier is a problem down there, or it certainly was at the time, in 2014. I think they did address it a little bit for the Olympics, but it was a problem. We arrived late the Friday night before the race and I realised that the next morning we had to get to this technical meeting to pick up numbers, and I didn't know how the heck we were going to do it. I couldn't make out any of the race information on the website work for me in the hotel bedroom.

I thought *Right, we'll try this guy Yuri.* I rang him at home and he said yes, he could be there. He took me to the race meeting, he did all the interpretation for me, and he made sure that his friend picked me up and got me to the race start. They were wonderful. The start was twenty-six miles outside Rio and you were running back into Rio, so it wasn't a question of just going to some square in Rio and setting off and coming back, it was quite difficult. So I got to the elite start and set off in the race with the elite runners. It was very hot and humid and I wasn't in the best shape to be running because the stress of what had been going on and the reason for me being out there had really taken a lot out of me. I was absolutely stunned when I came top ten in that race because that was a massive result. There was a lot of publicity in Rio for it because it is the biggest race in South America.

So, I did what I wanted to do out there, I broke my world record—by about two and a half hours actually—and it was amazing. But the problem was, when you are doing a world record you have to have a lot of endorsed information after it from race organisers proving that yes it was actually Fiona, yes she did actually run the race and yes we've actually got pictures of her at various points along the race, doing this race. Otherwise, basically you could put somebody in there to run part of it for you, you could cheat and it wouldn't be a proper world record.

And naturally that is taken very seriously by the Guinness World Record. To actually have your picture in the Guinness Book of World Records is quite a big thing of course.

We left the paperwork with the race organisers because we were flying home that Sunday afternoon after the race so Martin could go to work. And when we got back, I don't really know why, but we again hit this barrier when trying to get them to rubber stamp all the information for Guinness. Bless him, Yuri actually took it upon himself to make it happen and he did, he chased everybody up and we got it all authenticated.

That is always a massive worry. That's one of my main worries, doing these marathons—people think, oh it's just a marathon, go and run it and shut up. It's not like that. So much can go wrong. You've got to make sure that you've got all the correct information provided, the paperwork signed, endorsed, you've got to have the photographs, the video of you running—you've got to have all that. For example, a few years ago in October Callum Hawkins broke the Scottish national half marathon record. Only to be told in January it doesn't count because they didn't measure the course right and it's two hundred meters short. Even at that level, the biggest race in Scotland, an international race where national records are depending on it.

This happens quite a lot—they find out through people running with Garmins, they're coming back with feedback that it's not the full distance. I know it sounds ludicrous and you'd think the first thing you'd do if you were organising a marathon or half marathon is *make sure you've got the distance right*. But it happens quite a lot, so you're constantly worrying *Is it going to be validated, can I get this authenticated, can I make sure in the middle of running and the furore of travelling I've got all this documentation?* So Yuri got all the documentation for me, he was absolutely wonderful, a real friend, somebody that did for me at that point what I'd been going along doing for other people. Voluntarily stepped up and helped me. And it really makes you feel important. We'd have been lost without that, we would have invested all this money going to Rio and not been able to get the documentation that we needed.

So on the other side of the coin that just shows you it makes such a difference, the way you conduct your life towards others, both animals and people.

CHAPTER 32

Seven-Seven-Seven

I CAME BACK FROM THE Rio Marathon in July. I'd got my world records, I'd now broken my own record, and I had come top ten in this big international marathon even though I wasn't prepared for it. I thought *Okay, what's next?* I thought I'd just settle down for a while, look after the sanctuary. I'd do the publicity, I'd do some public speaking, but always, always, my job here at the sanctuary is to make sure this place runs, and that is a full time job and a half.

But coming up in February someone I knew from the North Pole marathon was getting a group together for this seven-seven-seven round the world challenge, to be authenticated by Guinness World Records. It would be seven marathons in seven days on seven continents. The question was, was I fit for it?

I figured the best way to actually address this distance-wise was probably to do a dummy run. I obviously couldn't run seven proper

194

marathons on seven consecutive days on seven continents as practice—logistically it's just not possible. I couldn't go to seven continents, that's a given. I couldn't find seven proper marathons to run back to back in seven days because there aren't any, but I could run six marathon distances consecutively and then on the seventh day do a proper marathon—in the UK, obviously, as I didn't want to be away for long. So I looked and found a marathon that was relatively local, wasn't too far to travel. The week before that marathon I ran six marathon distances from home whilst doing the sanctuary jobs. I made myself get up on the seventh day and go and run this marathon, and that was great. Despite the fact that I couldn't find the bloomin' thing and it was a bit of a palaver beforehand, because the marathon distance I'd run the day before, on Saturday, I'd actually run really late because we had an emergency with one of the horses that morning.

Because of that I had to drive straight to the marathon in the morning and it was atrocious weather, it was absolutely brutal. I remember thinking *What am I doing? Should I just not do this?* This marathon, the Stevenage Marathon, is a quite special marathon actually because it's only held once every ten years (there's a half marathon every year, but the full marathon is only every decade). So I ended up making myself do it and I won it with a 3:06:47 time. After that I figured right, this is good. I'm obviously fit enough and the distances and the banging on my legs is not too much of a problem. I can knock out a three-hour marathon after doing six marathons and the sanctuary job so I probably can cope with the actual travelling bit of this challenge if I push myself.

The problem was in the organisational side of this seven-seven-seven thing.

Another group of runners were also going to try and do this stunt of seven marathons on seven continents on seven consecutive days, only

195

they weren't going for a world record—and they'd waited for us to release the dates of when we were going to attempt this seven-day challenge and organised their challenge to occur the week before. At that point we couldn't change when we were going to do it, our races had to be authenticated. Our marathons had to be properly organised marathons where runners from host countries could enter. They were going to be races that were open to the public, and everything on our end had to be specially arranged for this challenge. This other group's races were simply going to be marathon distances on seven continents in seven days. If you think about it, if you pile off a plane and your job is to just run 26.2 miles, you can literally go to a park near the airport, Garmin yourself 26.2 miles, go back to the airport, get on your plane, and go to your next destination.

In contrast, we had to actually meet the criteria of being on race starts at declared times. We thought that's what Guinness required. They had to be proper races. It couldn't just be some 26.2 distance. And there is an awful lot of difference between the two things. But I figured the difference wouldn't be clear in the minds of the public. What I mean when I say 'race a marathon', is going and laying your heart and soul out on that tarmac for that length of time. Running a marathon distance is completely different. It's something I would not think too much about doing every Sunday in training. It is a completely different science.

But it was clear to me this other group was going to garner the publicity for the challenge. I was uncertain it would work out for us. Still, there had been promise that a documentary team would follow our group of runners. So I thought, *It's still positive for the animals. It is a challenge, whether we'll be the first ones to do it or not. I'll go along with it—I've said I'll do it. I will do it.* Then, the documentary team pulled out. I think they pulled out purely because they got wind of the fact that technically we weren't going to be the first group of runners to do this challenge.

So again I was left asking myself if it was actually worth putting myself through it. It would be a lot of pressure and stress to do it.

Ultimately I decided to go ahead and do it. But I thought *If I'm doing it, I'm not wasting my time.* And the only thing I could think of at the very last minute to make this slightly different or possibly worthwhile was to do it in fancy dress. Because I knew that none of the other group had done it in fancy dress, and certainly none of the lot I was doing it with were doing it in fancy dress.

So then it was emergency cow suit. Where do you get a cow suit that you can pack and wear to run a marathon every day, that's going to hold up to the rigors of this every day for a week—in less than two days? There was no way it could be customised to fit me, it was going to have to be something I could just buy off the rack.

So the two days before we're scheduled to leave I'm ringing around shops, asking, 'Have you got a cow suit? No, I don't want a big wooly one, have you got anything that's a little bit less?' I resorted to trawling the internet, and eventually found a cow suit that didn't really fit me, but did the job—it essentially was a cow, fancy dress. Keeping in mind I would have to run in temperatures right down to freezing in Punta Arenas or below in Antarctica, but in Abu Dhabi, where we would be running the Asian leg, it would be over 40 degrees. So it had to be an adaptable cow suit. I ordered a couple, actually. I looked them over and thought *Yeah, okay it's a goer.* Flew off to Australia, and funny enough, the cow suit is actually what saved the day for me, because CNN sent a film crew to Abu Dhabi and Paris, to actually film me doing it, purely because of the cow suit. So I did kind of salvage something back from that crisis. Just by thinking of something that I could do to make this a little bit different and garner attention for the animals.

But back to the races. We flew off to Melbourne and I arrived the night before the challenge started. We got up the next day. We ran our marathon in Melbourne. We got back on the plane. We flew to Abu Dhabi. That was a long flight, about 13 hours. We got off the plane, we ran our marathon in Abu Dhabi, which was terribly hot, naturally. Then we got back on the plane and we flew to Paris. We were really, really short for time in Paris because we were delayed. So I had to come through customs in Paris dressed in the cow suit. I don't know what they made of me, but they let me through.

We went off and ran our marathon in this park in Paris. I remember it was very cold in Paris. Then we got back on the plane and we flew to Tunis. Tunis was a complete and utter nightmare. We had to run in the middle of the night. The organisation was just everywhere. To be fair to them, they had really tried to make a big spectacle. They were desperate at the time for tourism in Tunis, with the Arab Spring uprising and everything. They were desperate to buoy their economy with tourism, so they made quite a big thing. The mayor was there and various officials were there to greet us. And we did the marathon. Then a few weeks after there was a terrible massacre, a terrorist massacre exactly where we had been running. It could so easily have been us. It brings it home to you.

Then we got back on the plane and we flew into Rome, and then on to New York. New York was brutal. I was getting depleted. I'd taken spare food for the countries where I thought there wouldn't be vegan food, but I hadn't taken a massive amount with me, thinking that some vegan food would be provided along the way. And it wasn't. So I was using the spare food that I'd brought in countries where I thought there would be vegan food and it turned out there wasn't. So I was getting really, really short. And the energy levels to do this challenge are extremely demanding. I was getting worn down.

We got off the plane, we went off into a park in New York, and we attempted to run. But it was so cold. It was the wintertime and it was icy and runners were slipping all over the place. Somebody broke their leg. We only just managed to fly out of New York before they grounded all the flights because of the blizzards.

Then the long flight down to Santiago, and then down to Punta Arenas. And we were delayed. We were heavily delayed. When we arrived in Punta Arenas, on Friday at four o'clock, we went to the hotel, and I remember them saying, 'Be ready to run at five.' And it was like, what, a marathon? Are you kidding? But we did it. We ran the sixth leg of the marathons along the seafront. And everybody was buoyant. They were so pleased. We got the okay, then, to get on the plane in Punta Arenas about midnight, and fly out to King George Island in Antarctica, where we would be able to land and run the seventh marathon.

It was absolutely incredible. It was exciting at that point. We'd gone through a lot. To even logistically make sure that your flights allow you to be able to do this chain of events and to stay well enough was an incredible accomplishment.

So we flew. We'd been flying for about two hours to King George Island. Beautiful, clear day. And then all of a sudden, we felt the plane turn. And people started going why are we turning? We can see the island down there. We should be landing. And the pilot came out and said, 'We're not landing, we're taking you back to Punta Arenas'. And it was like what? I remember just the hysteria on the plane. We didn't know what was really going on. We thought it was a joke. My recollection from when I was talking to people when I was stranded in Antarctica the time before—and I'd done a lot of talking to people obviously—was that they do not send the plane out if they do not know it can land. Purely because things like aviation fuel are expensive. They don't waste that kind of money. So I was saying they wouldn't have taken off if they didn't think it was going to be fit to land there. It's like less than two hours away.

It was maddening. Absolutely maddening. Steve, one of the other runners, was just gone frantic. He said, 'For some reason the pilot has just come out and said he won't land, and he's taking us back'. We just sat there completely numb. We were literally within an hour or two of being able to set off and run and complete this world record, and now we were turning around without even stepping foot on the continent.

We got back to Punta Arenas and the mood completely deflated. We were just devastated. It didn't make any sense. Everybody just went off to their rooms.

I decided that I wasn't going to get beaten by this, so I went back out in the cow suit, on my own. And I ran my last marathon on the coast that we'd run the night before. The Punta Arenas leg. Just basically to collect my thoughts and to affirm that at least I've done these seven distances, even if I haven't been allowed the privilege of doing it on this last continent in this time scale. That was Saturday afternoon.

I stayed in Punta until Tuesday waiting to hear if we could fly to Antarctica again or not. And in the end, the pressure again was on me to come home because Martin could lose his job. There's a finite time I can be away. I've always got to get back to the sanctuary, and I've got to get back well enough to do the work. I can't get back and be lying in my bed demanding hot tea and toast. I have to be well enough to put my clothes on and go outside and do heavy, hard work. I can't come back a shadow of the person I left. And so I decided, and I told the rest of the group that I was cutting my losses and going, because there was no world record there. Of course another problem was that even if we did go to Antarctica, we could potentially get stranded there. I couldn't do that again. I would be throwing away my sanctuary. Because if Martin lost his job, we'd have no money to run it. I couldn't put the animals at risk. It would be defeating the reason I was there.

So I came home from that, and I was utterly disheartened. Because it felt like another thing that had been snatched out from under me.

It was a big letdown. Especially going over Antarctica, seeing King George Island, being able to practically touch it, and then having to come back. It is really difficult to keep lifting yourself up from these things. I flew back from South America very disappointed and drained. It's not the running. It's the flying, and the logistics, and the stress, and the disappointment. They do all compound on you, and it brings it home to you that this is a pretty extreme way of living your life. I think a lot of people who run, basically the running that's the job and then they get some free time when they're not running. They get some life when they're not running. For me, when I'm not running I'm working. So there isn't any free time. There's no downtime. I've got to make my time back up at the sanctuary. So I think to myself, well this is a very, very high price to be paying for this running.

I came back to the UK. There's always a lot to do at the sanctuary so I got busy with that. And then I thought, *Well, what do I do next?* And that was when I decided I'd just do 100K in fancy dress.

CHAPTER 33

Race to the Stones (in a Cow Suit)

I HAD SOME PROBLEMS WITH my right knee at that point and I wasn't sure that it was going take to a road marathon. There is little road racing you can do, in terms of marathons, unless you go international. And even then, July's not really the time. So I thought, being as I'm not doing much and I'm just twiddling my thumbs, I'll go off and do this Race to the Stones. The Race to the Stones is the biggest ultra in the UK, so it has a high profile.

I intended to do another race in the fall, and I thought I'd just hone my skills a bit with the 100K. I had intended to run with this woman who was a lot slower than me. And Mike Julian, who'd run MDS on chemotherapy, he was going to be there. He was fully recovered now. And another one of my compatriots from the 2012 MDS, Jason Nash, who was inspired to go vegan from being around me in 2012 and has actually stayed vegan up until this present day, he was running too.

I told them that if we were going to run round and muddle about and whatever together, I'd just do it for strength. Because my knee wasn't great, I wasn't sure it was going to take the pounding of a road marathon. My plan was to stay with them, but I'd run in my cow suit, because I didn't like to waste the opportunity. There's no point drudging along. I can as easily drudge along in a cow suit and at least raise a few eyebrows or get the message out to one or two people. Things that you can often do better when you've got a little bit more time. You don't talk to people when you're running a fast road marathon. But when you're actually in a longer distance race, you've got more chances for a bit of conversation, and there'll be questions about why you're doing what you're doing. You can get your point over. And if you're doing well, then you're actually physically communicating your message. You are the manifestation of what you're saying you can do.

So we went over to the Cotswolds, where the Race to the Stones is. It was July, and the hottest day of the whole year. I turned up, there's a flood of runners, and I met the others that I was going to run with—to a point. We couldn't really run together, because it's really, really hard to run in a group. That was the difficulty when we were doing those seven-seven-seven marathons all chained together. Everybody wanted a toilet break at a different time. I mean some of the guys that were not getting on so well, they were out of their comfort zone in that race and they had to stop for chips. I've never stopped for chips in a marathon before. We stopped for chips in Tunis in the middle of the night. I'm thinking, *What are we doing?*

So it's extremely hard to gauge a pace that's going to be comfortable for all, over that kind of distance. But the plan was we'd meet up and we'd have a laugh together. And we'd be bound to be yo-yoing each other on the course, if any of us felt like running together. So we turned up, and

I hadn't told them I was going through my cow suit phase. So it's like 'Oh my lord, cow suit no, pretend you don't know her'. One of the race organisers saw me and said, 'You're not intending to run the whole thing in that are you?'

'Yes'.

And he said, 'But you're stopping overnight, right?' Because in this 100 kilometer race, you can actually stop midway at 50K. A couple of the people in my group did intend to do that, have a little bit of a rest and then carry on the last 50K the next day. It's a hard race. 100K is quite a long way to run at the best of times, and the terrain out there isn't ideal. But I said to the race organiser, 'No, no. I'm going to run the whole thing. I've got to get back anyway because my mum's waiting for me'. She was waiting for me at the finish and I didn't want her to be there all night.

But they tell you to take a head torch and a jacket and provisions for when it gets dark. So of course, I've got my cow suit on and then I've got to wear a giant pack with all this extra stuff that they've told us we'd need because it's going to be dark when you finish. And I thought well obviously I'm in my cow suit and I've got this dodgy knee so it may take me awhile, so I better pack it all. I don't want to be fumbling my way around the Cotswolds in the dark. That's not going to work out, is it?

So I set off at the back of the race with my friends, where the more inexperienced and less quick runners are going to be. I knew I wasn't going to be that quick, because I hadn't trained for it. And again, I'm wearing a cow suit. But unfortunately the race started on a very narrow path. The front runners went off and I didn't want to be a front runner, I didn't want to be standing shoulder to shoulder with really good ultrarunners, and I'm dressed as a cow. It looks like you're just taking the mick. So I stayed at the back with my friends and we chatted and we kind of wended our way through. We'd lost a lot of ground, but I was actually running a bit quicker than them, so I thought well I better do what my knee is dictating to me. Because if I'm feeling a bit of pain in my knee, sometimes if I run too slow I'll feel more pain.

We went through a very wooded section with a lot of tree roots, and it was quite dark. And this one guy had been trying to get past me for ages. I don't really know why. I can only assume that he did not like running behind a woman dressed as a cow. But he made a pass to try and get around me at the absolute most inappropriate point he could have done. And instead of getting round me, he fell on top of me and brought me down. Which was a bit of a disaster, because he landed with his full weight and I was on my right stride, my weight all on my right knee. I just crumbled.

My leg gave way underneath me, took a knock on one of the tree roots, and the minute I stood up and tried to bend it, it really hurt, hurt terribly. I managed to get to the checkpoint at 20K, another three miles up the road, and I noticed that one or two other people had fallen in this very treacherous dark wooded area with a lot of tree roots. A lot of people seemed to have got knee injuries, and the doctor seemed to be applying this kinetic tape to them. So I asked if they could give me some of this tape, and the doctor looked at it and told me no, obviously you've had surgeries, what we don't want to do is put something on it that is going to make it worse for you. I couldn't really start, that would need to be something case specific to your leg. The only thing we can do is, if your leg's swollen, take painkillers, if you want to continue. But in view of the fact there's another 80K, perhaps you would consider not continuing on, or you get to 50K and then rest, and go into the full medical tent there.

Not very good. So I went on to the next checkpoint at 30K, and asked again, can I have some of the pink tape? It was the same thing the other doctor had told me. No, you can't. Okay. But I had an emergency piece of Tubigrip, which is like a surgical stocking thing that I'd thought I might need. So I put that on and it was quite painful, so I did take some painkillers that they gave me. But unfortunately I'm not used to taking painkillers, I never normally would do that and it was just a question of do you pull out, or do you see if you can finish? And I'm not big into pulling out, because always, always, always I'm very aware that despite the fact that I have got this bad knee, and I have had a guy fall on top of me, and it is not my fault, generally speaking when anything negative happens with a vegan, it becomes public knowledge, and of course people would think I couldn't cut it because I'm vegan.

I decided I wanted to try and continue. It wasn't the end of the world pace-wise, it was just that I had to overcome the pain, which did settle at a certain level of just about tolerable. So I got into the 50K halfway point, where the big tent is, with bands playing and everybody's sort of all jolly and thinking about camping down or whatever they were doing.

I went to the fridge for a drink, and I'd been told there would be vegan food. Certainly there was an enormous amount of food available in this tent. But I went to the fridge and I looked and it was full of milk. They had every sort of milk you can possibly imagine—and beyond what you could imagine, things I've never heard of, lactose intolerant, semi-skimmed, whatever, everything was in there. And I asked one of the girls who were serving, do you have any soya milk? And after we'd battled through the 'What? Semi-skimmed?' 'No, soya' exchange, the answer was no, we don't have that here. The attitude was like it was some alien product, and I was an absolute nuisance and beast for asking for it. I decided well that really isn't right, that is completely and utterly wrong. I looked at the rest of the food that was available and it was all cakes and stuff that quite clearly weren't vegan. It angered me a little bit. So I thought I don't want to stop, I want the job done, I want to get to the destination. And so I figured well I'll carry on. I don't like to stop very much when I'm running, even if it's a longer distance. So I continued on without anything from the tent; there was nothing really I could eat there. I had a few bars I'd baked myself so I had a nibble of that and just continued on. And I thought, well okay, this is not ideal, I wasn't in an ideal shape when I started, probably, but I'm really not in an ideal shape now. But I'm always, always trying to salvage something out of everything I do.

I decided to use the experience as a sort of benchmark to test exactly what people's reaction is to veganism. I did this at the checkpoints: I was running into these checkpoints every 10K, and I was actually climbing the field, I was quite high in the race at this point. It was baking hot and I was passing a lot of runners who were absolutely flagging at the side of the road, and although my knee was bad, once I got that under control, it was manageable—in terms of the fact that if I can tolerate it for several hours, it's not getting any worse, it's just hurting. I just have to accept that this knee is going to hurt.

And so I ran into checkpoints. If you run into a checkpoint you get a big, 'Come on the lady in the cow suit, you're doing brilliantly well, blimey you're really flying, you're catching runners, you're doing massively well, and you're wearing a cow suit and it's so hot'. If I ran in and they asked 'Why you wearing a cow suit? You should be concentrating on making better time'. I said, 'Well I'm raising funds for my animal sanctuary'. And the response was 'Oh brilliant, you've got an animal sanctuary?' 'Yeah, we've got 400 rescued animals'. 'Oh wow, you go on then, I hope you raise a lot'. So the next checkpoint I run into I get the same question of course, 'Why you wearing a cow suit?' And if I said 'I'm wearing it to show solidarity for cattle, particularly dairy cows who are suffering in an industry which is exploiting them, exploiting their babies, and they have no voice, and I'm a vegan, and I want to show that support in a visible way'...it's like dead silence. I'm not saying anybody said it, but I'm sure they were thinking it: 'Well I think you're stupid, and I hope you go and drop dead'. That kind of thing. It just was like, Okay then. Goodbye.

And it was that kind of negativity, that kind of brick wall unwillingness to engage that I found along the way, that's what happened when I did the North Pole. The BBC asks the perfectly logical question, 'Why did you run a marathon at the North Pole?' and do you say 'I'm a lunatic'? You're not going to say that. Do you say 'I'm an adrenaline junkie that just loves doing these harebrained things, because it's just so much fun'? That, they would have been very receptive to. If I'd have said, 'I'm doing it to raise funds for Help for Heroes', if I'd said I was doing it to raise funds for a human track-based charity, I think then they would've grabbed hold of it. But when you're saying 'I'm doing it to promote veganism in a positive way', it's just completely negative. People are completely shut down to it, they don't want to know, they want you to go away, just get rid of her.

So I'm chugging along and I come into the next stop and I realise I got to the finish. My mum was waiting for me, and it wasn't even dark. And my first reaction was to think, *Ohh* poo. *I've carried all these head torches, and all this clothing for after dark when it's going to get cold, and I've finished and it isn't even dark yet.* It was annoying. So I've not only just finished in my cow suit on this hottest day of the year, I finished in what we call an elite time, where you finish before dark, which I never anticipated might happen. So I'd carted a great big pack full of things I didn't need with me. You might ask 'Well why didn't you get rid of them at 50K or whatever? You obviously knew you were going to finish'. Yes, but you don't throw away a head torch that cost 60 pounds—I don't anyway. I had to keep it with me. It's like at the end of the Marathon de

Sables, in the last stage, I'm the only runner who's keeping hold of her pack and her stove and everything. I paid for it, I don't want to throw it away, I'm sorry I just don't want to, it's not in me to want to waste something like that.

So I got into the finish of the Race to the Stones, and finished twelfth.

I paid a high price for that race. I was not dehydrated when I finished running, but I could not rehydrate afterwards, because my stomach was rejecting everything; I think because I'd taken some painkillers. My stomach would not absorb anything. We were in a hotel that night and we intended to go home the next morning, but as the night wore on I got worse and worse and worse, I became more and more dehydrated, to the point where my mum sought help in the hotel.

Fortunately, (we thought), there was a conference of doctors staying at the same hotel, but we asked somebody and he said 'We can't help you—we're not medical doctors, we're researchers'. So we called a paramedic who came out, and he said to just keep sipping water and try to rehydrate. And I knew that that wasn't going to happen, but he said if you really want to go to A&E, you can get a taxi to an A&E, but just keep trying to rehydrate. And I couldn't, and then all of a sudden I just started vomiting in front of him, and he said, 'Get an ambulance'.

I went to A&E and waited, and as soon as the doctor came down and learned I did a lot of sport, she took one look at me and said 'Right, I want four and half litres of fluid into her, and she'll be back up and bouncing around'.

But I did have an episode when they put me on a pulse monitor, during the part when they leave you in a little curtained area and they ask you what you've been doing. My mum was saying 'She's run this 100K, she's done it in a cow suit', blah blah blah. The intake nurse said, 'Oh she must be fit then'. So normally they set the pulse rate monitor at 60 beats a minute, and if it goes below that then it sets off an alert and the nurses come to make sure you're all right. So they said, being as she's really fit we'll put hers at 50 beats a minute, so anything below that's a problem, but above 50 that's going to be okay. So sure enough, as my pulse rate starts to drop when I got fluids in, my pulse rate went to below 50 beats a minute, the alerts went off, and all the medical crash crew came in. I told them 'Look, it's fine, I've got quite a low pulse', so the doctor said, 'Okay, we'll put it 40, and then that covers all eventualities'.

So they went away, and I was desperately trying to convince this one doctor that I was all right, and could go, and he was pretty satisfied with that. He'd just gone off when a cardiologist from one of the medical wards said he wanted to come down and see me. I could hear his voice in the corridor, and all of a sudden these alerts went off again. My pulse had gone below 40. And they ran in with a crash crew to get my heart going again, and I'd been given a bit of toast at this point, so I'm sitting over there in bed, feeling all embarrassed because there's all this furore and curtains being thrown open, and doctors rushing in for an emergency and I'm sitting here eating a piece of toast. Fortunately that doctor was a senior cardiologist, and he said, she's fit, she's going to have her pulse below 40, thirty-odd is really rare, it's really unusual, but not when you look at what she's doing. So I got the okay to leave.

Then it was just a matter of going home and recovering. I recover very quickly. That's the one thing people need to know about sport. It's not necessarily how much you can do in one given training session, it's how quickly you can recover from that and be ready to do it very quickly on the next one. That is going to give you the enhanced performance. I think that's what people don't understand, almost certainly with drugs in long distance sport. Yes, drugs cheaters have beaten me, and it really hurts. It really hurts when you get placings in races that you know would have been a lot higher if you take out the high profile runners at the top end that have been disqualified. When you've got a place lower down that would've been higher without the cheaters, you start looking at the lists of the ones that have won and thinking, well take away that one, take away that one—my placing really rises quite significantly.

But what I think people need to realise is, the drugs, especially for long distance, don't actually make people go quicker. They allow you to train longer, and more intensely, *so* that you can go quicker. And that means that they allow you to recover quicker. So when you're not taking anything, you're relying on a very fit and strong body to repair itself quickly, to recover, to get out and do the next session. And I think that is a testament in itself to the plant-based lifestyle, which I have led for a very long time and that continues to allow me to do this.

And to a certain extent the same applies to my mum, who travels with me. She's been with me there and back to Australia in less than four days, she's been up a volcano at 14,400 feet, administering to people who are in their 20s that can't cope up there.

The bizarre juxtapositions that we've been in with these races. I mean even when I was doing the road races, I'd literally turn up with my mum. There'd be coaches and physios surrounding the other runners in the technical meetings for instance, and I'd be feeling embarrassed because I wasn't taking notes. I'd be sitting at the back of the room playing noughts and crosses with my mum, trying to make it look like I'm doing something other than panicking or just feeling like a complete and utter imposter, like I just didn't belong there.

And you know I still don't understand that much about running. I know about training, but I'm not an expert. Some of the technical conversations I'd overhear or people would try to engage me in—I just don't know. It's really difficult. I've been in the top races with the best of the best. I don't know how I've got there, perhaps it's been my naivety, not really comprehending the extent of what I'm doing. I've always found it very difficult to train alone around here, to literally have nobody in my family who understands sports. Martin, he goes along with it, he knows I do it, but for instance he's never seen me run. He knows I *can* run, he's seen me on the treadmill, he's seen me leaving the house to train and as far as he's concerned I've gone to run, but he hasn't seen me race. They don't understand the ludicrousness of what I've done. And perhaps that's what's always kept me grounded. It's just always been some surreal thing that happens two weekends a year, and then I come back to total normality.

I remember being at the airport in Berlin one year after doing the Berlin Marathon, one of the biggest races in the world, with nearly 50 thousand runners. And I met somebody who was flying back to the UK, and she said she's from a running club that I know, and she said, 'Oh, that was a hard race, heart racing. How did you do?' And I said, 'Oh, yeah I came 17th'. And she kind of looked at me as if she might have heard wrong. 'What, in the race?' And I said yes. She's like, 'What! In the Berlin Marathon?' And it's like, but that's ludicrous! That's like world class, that's the best runners in the world. It's the race where the world record gets broken. People get phenomenal times in this race. For me it's just the job I've set myself to do. I only want to do as well as I thought I could do setting out. It's never been that special, it's just been the best I could do. I don't flatter myself that it's any better than it is, but these things are a big deal to people, and the medals and the trophies mean a lot to them. People accuse me of being cavalier, and I probably do brush my results aside, but it's because I don't actually want to go back and revisit those experiences.

Brushing it all aside is my way of coping with how difficult it actually has been. When I go to an event, I will be laughing, I will be joking, I'll be mucking around, but when the race head goes on it's not the Fiona that anybody would recognise when they actually see me out there. I am completely focused on what I'm doing, and there is no laughing and smiling. It is intensely important to me to do as well as I can. That's the job that's got to be done. And once I've done it that's it, I'm on to the next thing. What's the next challenge? What's the next angle?

The only reason I really took to running was that I realised that no matter how much I can introduce people to the sanctuary and show them the animals here, and show people how they interact with each other, and show how wrong it is to exploit them in any way, shape or form, people will say, 'Yes, but that's your opinion Fiona; you are a no one. And we don't want to listen to a no one'. So in order to get your message across you've got to become a someone. Every race I do is like physically knocking another nail into that platform to erect some sort of place I can speak from, a place where people actually want to listen. Usually people want to listen because you've done something that they respect, admire, or would like to do themselves. So yes, I've done the elite road running, and I've done the Marathon des Sables three times, the North Pole, Antarctica, the Atacama Desert, I've done a 100K while dressed in a cow suit, I've done seven marathons in seven days on six continents, dressed as a cow. I've done a lot of things very far outside the ordinary, basically because people are interested in hearing about extraordinary things. And then the natural progression is to ask, 'And how do you make this happen?' And it's really funny actually when people ask me, 'What's the trick?'

It hurts. It really hurts to do the training. And it's a classic cliché, but the trick is to not mind that it hurts. So my trick is that I don't mind how much pressure I put on myself, I don't mind how much effort I personally put into something, because I feel it's doing a little bit of good for the animals. And that's where the rewards have been. Not in the times and trophies and medals or whatever—in doing some good on behalf of the animals.

Probably it does sound like this wonderful, exciting thing, that I've been continent hopping and had all these experiences that could look glamorous from a distance. But it's not like that at all. My heart is here at the sanctuary, doing the grassroots care. Always has been and always will be. The rest is just something I've done as an extra thing.

I've done it as an amateur, but I only know how to do things full on. Otherwise I'm not going to waste my time bothering. I don't spend a lot on my diet, I don't take any supplements and I don't have anything case specific for running. It's a very bland, basic lifestyle. I wouldn't say I've run particularly from my body, which isn't that ideal and suitable for the sport—I've run from my heart and my mind. It's how I do everything. I do it 100 percent and it gets the results, I hope.

So you've got to be very careful and those disappointments do start to eat away at you. You feel that all you're doing is running in an endless race and when you get to the finish they say 'Actually, Fiona, could you go and run another five miles?' And you do it, like a little Duracell bunny, and you get to that point and then they say, 'Could you go and run another five?' And it's absolutely hard pulling it together, it really is. Because these are monumental efforts—I know I sometimes sound very casual and blasé about what I've done, because I realise that I am an insignificant speck of sand in a massive universe and there isn't a lot of good going on out there. But it takes every ounce of everything I've got to do it. I feel ashamed sometimes, that I haven't been able to do more, but I really haven't, I've tried it every way around, I've been an angry young abolitionist, I've been that person wanting to climb on top of Nelson's

Column and shout, and grab people and say, Why aren't you seeing what I am seeing? Why aren't you making this connection between sufferings? Why can't you see?

It's a question I still don't understand the answer to.

CHAPTER 34

The 4 Deserts

AFTER THE RACE TO THE STONES I looked round for things to do, and I decided to do the 4 Deserts Ultramarathon Series race, which is basically a four stage race. You run a race in the Gobi Desert, the Antarctic, the Atacama Desert, and then it used to be the Sahara but that was deemed too dangerous so now it's the Namibian desert. Each one is 250K. The challenge started in May, with the Namibian race first up. I figured these races weren't as brutal as Marathon des Sables by any stretch, but there's four of them, so I had to be careful. Self-sufficiency for a week, and a similar sort of distance, but there's little things that you don't have to supply that make a big difference. For instance, there's plenty of water, so you can wash, and there's facilities like toilets and stuff like that, so it's not as tough.

So I'd planned to go off to Namibia, but I had a terrible time before I went and nearly decided not to go. Purely because we lost two horses at the sanctuary; a mother and a son who were very closely bonded and I'd had in my care for over twenty-two years, since they came from Russia, and it took me apart.

The way it happened was that Marsha, the mare, had been ridden from Russia 22 years ago by a lady who'd written a book about it. She was a very wealthy woman whose husband had sponsored the trip. Unbeknownst to them at the time, Marsha was pregnant, and as soon as she arrived, she dropped her foal, Ashipka. After a few months, the wealthy woman and her husband went their separate ways, and the husband was left with Marsha and this foal Ashipka. I knew him through my work at the stock exchange and he asked me to take them. I did, and they stayed with me for over twenty years.

They never left each other's side. As Marsha became older, she started to need a stable at night, but Ashipka used to follow her into her stable to make sure she was safe, and then he'd wander back out to the rest of the herd. Same thing in the morning, I'd open the gate to go out and feed, Ashipka would wander in to collect his mum, and they'd go out together. But Marsha became lame and she couldn't get out. We didn't know what was wrong her leg, but anybody who knows about horses knows that with the limbs of a horse—horses generally are not designed to be fixed, they are designed to be well and then obviously if they aren't well in a natural environment, they fall and then predators prey on them. They don't react well to surgeries, they don't react well to illness generally. Certainly not of the limbs; you must keep a horse on all four limbs, the bigger the horse the more important it is.

Marsha was a relatively big horse. She couldn't come out, so I let Ashipka in, to come and see her. He came and visited his mum, all through that day. And his mum got worse. We could not get her up, she could not stand up. The critical point is a horse can't be down for more than 15 hours or so, or all the arteries in the rump get squashed, and they get a dead leg. They literally can't support their own weight if they're down too long. The following day came and Marsha still couldn't get up. We had all sorts of veterinary intervention, but they could not work out what was wrong, why her leg was just not working for her, other than the fact that she was now very old. She went to the ground, she couldn't get up, and she had to be put to sleep. And even though we let Ashipka see exactly what had happened, he became very distressed that night, terribly distressed.

I rang the vet, and said, 'Look, Ashipka, her son, is really not taking this very well, he might need sedation'. The response was 'Don't be ridiculous, it's a horse'. I said he's a horse that has lost his mother, he has never been without his mother. This isn't just a distressed horse, this is really serious. The next morning came and it got worse, and the vet agreed, she said she'd come back out. She came back out and his pulse rate was all over the place, he'd become dehydrated. She left me with IV fluids for him and told me to get to a lorry and get him to the vet.

I got a lorry, got a girl to come with her lorry, and we got him just about on the lorry, and I looked at him and I thought *He doesn't want to go.* He just didn't want to be on that lorry and he didn't want to go to the vet. So I opened the back of the lorry, and he came off. He went into the stables, he checked every box, looked for his mum. I swear I've never seen anything like it, he went down to even the outdoor stables that we've got, and he looked over the doors, saw she wasn't in there, walked away. And then within an hour, he just literally went to the ground and died. We do not know what of. It was like he died of a broken heart. He knew what had happened. I've never seen anything like it. It broke my heart.

It broke my heart, because I'd lost Marsha and I'd lost Ashipka within the space of 24 hours. But more than that, it emphasised to me the bond these animals must have. What we must be doing to pigs in farrowing crates when we rip their babies from them. We have these stupid soap operas on television and you see some storyline where a mother loses her baby at twenty-three weeks, everyone talks about it. There's discussions on all these chat shows about how traumatic it is. And always in the back of my mind is yes, of course you feel compassion for that person. But how is it we feel no compassion for the calves that we rip from the cows? How is it that we find it acceptable to do that, to other sentient beings, but we can be so compassionate towards humankind. Or some of humankind, rather. We're not even that compassionate towards some of our fellow humans. I really can't make sense of it.

This all happened about two days before I was supposed to go to Namibia, so I wasn't in the best place when I went out there, mentally or emotionally. I just didn't want to go basically. Going through the motions in these races is not pleasant. I arrived out there and I just wasn't concentrating on the first day, I'm not going to pretend otherwise. I wasn't even looking where I was going, I don't think. I was in a daze. I'd spent like two days crying, I'd flown to Namibia, and the race just meant nothing to me. And the added difficulty was that before the race, South African Airlines lost my luggage, which had all my food in it. So I've got this race to do for a week and I've got no vegan food. I've had to go into Swakopmund and buy some nuts. I've got some nuts in my bag, and I'm thinking *I'm going to go into the desert and run like this on a bag of nuts?* Also in my luggage and thus also lost was my sleeping bag, which was synthetic, and the only thing I could replace it with was a down sleeping bag. I kept thinking *I don't want to do this, I don't want to be here.*

In the end I sourced a bit more and got a synthetic bag, even though it was massive, and shoved it all in this borrowed rucksack and got my cow suit. I had that with me, I obviously deemed that to be hand luggage.

Then, when I was about 4K into the race I tripped up. I simply wasn't looking where I put my feet, and I tripped up and fractured two ribs, like a fool. So now it was oh what have I done, what have I done now?

Funnily enough, as soon as the point came that I'd have to pull out, because I'd fractured two ribs, that gave me the reason to not want to pull out, the fact that I now had to.

I was really worried—I was kind of all right if I stood the right way, but I had a backpack on, and I had to climb and do all this ridiculous endurance running the race calls for, and I'd got this cow suit and tail to worry about. It was a nightmare. But now I did want to be there, because now I was facing the prospect of having to go home—and that was real failure. So I continued on with my fractured ribs. It was very painful, so I was doing this funny kind of running style, I don't know what I was doing. It was really hard to put the pack on in the morning. It wasn't so bad when I got it on, but oh, putting it on in the morning, every breath I took was awful. The long stage was particularly horrible. It was horrible weather, it was cold and it was truly brutal. And I'd not got the nutrition that I wanted to have because of the luggage being lost.

You get through it. I finished quite well actually, and the long stage didn't take me that long, maybe it wasn't that bad. I trundled through it in my cow suit, and you kind of lose yourself in this world where you can actually sink. Somebody had told me that if you're a bit down these races do a jolly good job of deflecting your attention. Because that's all you've got to focus on, finishing. It's not life and death, but to you it's very important. It was something different to focus on. It did distract me. So I pulled myself together for that, and then I was going to go off and do the next one, which was in the Gobi Desert. But in the end I didn't go to the Gobi race, because my parents were selling their house so that they could move into the sanctuary and get the money from their house to pay off the mortgage.

They were going to be moving the day I was supposed to be going to the Gobi Desert. And I just couldn't do it. I couldn't go, logistically no way was that going to happen. I'd had to help them move the week before, they hadn't even had a removal van, it was all done by hand. And then completing that and just saying 'Hi, move in here, there's a load of animals everywhere, it's not quite finished and I'll be off. I'm going to the Gobi Desert'—it simply wasn't going to work, and I decided that it wasn't possible to do the 4 Deserts that year.

Genuinely speaking, the death of two of the horses in that tragic way was not something I was ever going to shake off two days before that race in Namibia. It really wasn't. I was absolutely bereft and distraught. When the animals are ill I am there with them, I am not telling some young girl or lad to go down and see to them, I'm there with them, I've been there with them at their side for 22 years. I don't just vanish in the house and say, 'Oh well I've got a race to run'.

One year here we had such bad ice and snow there was no water outside. Every bucket of water the animals drank had to be carried from our utility room down to the stables, and it was taking me five or six hours just to do that one thing. You are there with them all the time, and you don't just switch it on and off; your heart is always there, and if anything goes wrong it can have a bigger, detrimental effect. That's where the psychology comes into it.

Your body activates when you get out there. It's life or death, get on with it. You've done it before, you can do it again, but it's whether your mind wants you to do it and wants you to push that bit extra. I get my biggest inspiration from my training and my preparation, and if you know what to expect, and you've been fit enough to address it in training, then I think you're going to do pretty well. But I find that psychological part of my running is the most important part. Because I'm doing it for a passion. I'm doing it for a belief. I want to help others, but I'm not ashamed to say that the ones here at the sanctuary are always at the forefront of my mind; they've got to be.

CHAPTER 35

Percy Bear

I'M GOING TO END THIS BOOK by talking about Percy Bear. As his name suggests, Percy is a little bear, and I carry him with me in all my races. He's small enough to fit in the palm of your hand. He started off as a sanctuary mascot. The work I do can be very sad, and it can be very intense in a negative way, in that yes, the animals we're looking after, they're fine. But the reason we have a sanctuary, the reason anybody has a sanctuary, is that most of the animals out there aren't fine. They're very far from fine. And that's the message I'm trying to convey to people with everything I do. It can be quite downbeat a lot of the time, so I figured we needed something to make it a little more upbeat. Percy is my alter ego, the cheeky little chap that can go where I can't, and say what I can't say, and do things that I can't myself.

When I started to do the more shall we say alternative races, such as Marathon des Sables, I suppose I wanted a little bit of company, and

223

a friendly face along the way. But also something that could help me convey a message. That's where Percy Bear came in. I had no idea how popular he would become, and how I would come to be identified with a little bear. That wasn't some grand plan. But as it's panned out, I realise that perhaps when you're trying to do your running with a purpose, an alternative message that people may be resistant to, it's kind of a sign saying, 'I'm non-threatening. I carry a small bear'. It breaks the ice and softens the situation so that you can to get your message across softly, rather than in a very hardline and aggressive way. It's not my style to be like that, so I have to do it in a way I feel comfortable with.

So Percy goes with me, and he's been absolutely everywhere. He started his adventures in the Marathon des Sables, and he's got the T-shirt, literally, to prove he's done it. He wears it all the time. It's a little under-vest. How he got that T-shirt is not a pretty story though. They were selling little bears at the expo after the event, and he stole it off one of them. He bought a little bear with a T-shirt on, and adapted it himself. That was the naughty side of Percy coming out there.

He went to the North Pole, and Antarctica, and if you look at footage of me crossing the finish line, I'm holding him. People actually ask, 'What's Percy up to next? What's he doing?' And when we were in Omsk a lot of the school children in the city were aware that we were coming, and primary school children had made little banners and pictures, and lined the course with 'Come On Percy Bear' signs.

I have a lot of other bears that have been sent to me. When I won the North Pole Marathon, I was so successful, and Percy was so successful. He was the first small teddy bear to run the North Pole Marathon. One guy set up the Percy Supporter Group, where everybody took to sending photographs of their bears cheering Percy on while I was doing the world record. I'd got my human supporters, and he had his little teddy bear supporters. A lot of people started to send me bears, so I keep them as his fan club, in the room I use as a gym.

He's a softer side, a funny side, an alternative side of the work I'm doing. So now people genuinely do write to him, and he's got his own Facebook page, and people actually do look out for him in races. We've had some really funny moments. In Marathon des Sables, when I was suffering terribly, as everyone was in 2012, there were some squaddies in the tent next door to me, some serious, serious soldiers, and every night they decided it was going to be really funny to hide Percy somewhere around the camp, and we'd have to go and look for him. The people in our tent were really suffering on our expedition, and we all wanted to lie down, and instead of getting to that we had to first go and look for Percy. It was tough, but funny. A way to distract yourself from the severity of the MDS experience.

So Percy goes everywhere with me now, a travelling companion. Prepping for MDS and everybody's counting in grams and Martin's chopped the little bits of foil off painkillers to try to save on weight, so I've got a bag full of loose painkillers because I'm not carrying that extra foil that holds them all together. And then, all of a sudden in goes Percy, and he's not that light. I think he's gaining weight. His scarf's quite heavy, but he does strip down, obviously. He just goes with his T-shirt on and his little bandana. But it's more important to me to carry him than leave him behind and have a slightly lighter pack.

Even when we've been travelling in places where there's a big language barrier, if you walk in and you're smiling sweetly and you've got a little teddy bear, people generally tend to smile no matter where you are. In the middle of Dubai Airport, when everybody's in a hurry, people see the bear and there's a look of surprise and then they smile.

Or for instance when we were in Russia. Russia is kind of a tricky place to travel through, but I've got a lot of friends out there, and a lot of people that I've helped out there. I remember one year I went to Russia and a lot of people had come to meet me at my hotel to thank me, with little gifts that they'd made or bought me, which was very humbling. But when we arrived at the airport to return home, the interpreter said, 'I just don't envy you trying to get through customs with that giant bag of whatever it is you've got there'. I had a big teddy, and little Percy and a bunch of other stuffed animals. And the airport staff were lovely with me. It was like, 'Yeah, yeah, go through.' In fact, somebody had bought me a big toy dog, and even the security man, who I thought was going to stop me and like pull me aside and say, 'What are you carrying that for?' he just said, 'Oh, you've got a big dog. Do you like dogs?' I said, 'Yes,' and he said, 'What you calling it?' I said, 'I don't know, what's your name?' And he said, 'Boris'. I said, 'Okay, I'll call him Boris,' and he was really thrilled. It's a way of breaking down some of our barriers.

It's been a talking point in interviews, something a little bit unusual, 'And tell us about the bear. Tell us why you carry him'. Also as an educational tool for much smaller children. Toddlers particularly love him, and we have had a few moments when toddlers have taken such a great fancy to him that it's been quite difficult to explain to a 16 month old that you can't keep him, as I'm running away with him.

After one stage in the Marathon des Sables, they give you a tiny little cup of mint tea. And even though it's a tiny little cup, teeny, teeny, because water and fluids, especially hot fluids, are so limited, you're looking at it as if you've got the greatest thing on the world. When I finished that stage, the Berber handing them out gave me one and he gave Percy one, and then this race organiser came over and said, 'No, she's only allowed one', and Percy's was snatched away.

But Percy will go in my pack, and people then ask you the question, 'Why are you carrying that little bear?' rather than you forcing something upon them. It's just a way of drawing people into the story, in a non-aggressive manner.

So I'm constantly thinking of these inventive ways to get my message home, even if it's just to a few people. Different things affect different people. For sure, for some people the more overt pushy hard approach might work; they have the facts explained to them and then their mindset allows them to say, 'Yes, I see. I realise. I understand and I don't want any part of that anymore'. But for large swaths of people you do have to be inventive to get through to them. Because very often, the minute that they go on the defensive, and perhaps they know you're right, they can become aggressive, and that's something that you don't want. Because with that aggression, the barrier goes up, the wall is built, and that gives them the excuse to walk away.

Because they do walk away, and the labels that they attach to you are, 'Oh you're crazy,' or 'You're just too extreme', and you don't want to appear to be that. You want to appear to be a very level-headed person. And what works for me now, is to be a level-headed person, to not even give them probably an inkling of the fact that I'm … *vegan*. Like, tell them about the sanctuary, my running, the things that I've done that they can actually respect, and then tell them this is how I've done it, and it might be of interest, and it might benefit them to do something similar. That's my way of approaching it.

I'm just an individual person who happens to believe something very, very deeply and very passionately, and I want to share it with others for their benefit, as well as the animals' benefit, as well as the environment's benefit. So, as I've said, you have to be inventive with your little bears, and your running, and whatever works to do that.

–End–

How You can Help

Running Tower Hill Stables Animal Sanctuary and providing care to over 600 residents is hugely expensive with feed bills alone often exceeding £15,000 a month.

If you would like to help Fiona, donations are greatly appreciated and all go directly towards helping animals in need. Please visit the website at www.towerhillstables.org and follow the "ways to help" link. We accept PayPal, Transferwise and direct account transfers.

Thank you so much. Everything helps. Even a small donation. You can also send Fiona a message at Fiona@towerhillstables.com or via Instagram @oakes.fiona and @towerhillstables.

To help Fiona with her vegan outreach program, please visit www. fionaoakesfoundation.com.